History of the Deep State Volume II

History of the Deep State, Volume 2

Jeremy Stone

Published by Jeremy Stone, 2020.

'History of the Deep State: Volume II'

JEREMY STONE

SECTION 6.3 Visions For 2022

HISTORY OF THE DEEP STATE VOLUME II

THIRTY-THREE

THE FIRST TEMPLE OF King Solomon stood for years. King David ruled Israel for 33 years. There are 33 vertebrae in the human spinal Colum. There are 33 degrees in the Old Masonic Order. Jesus rose on the third day at the age of thirty-three. The sun leaves the house of the zodiac at the 33rd degree. The original Knights of the round table had 33 seats, with the 33rd seat designated for the King. The U.N. Flag Map divides the earth into 33 sections. White Sands, New Mexico resides at the 33rd parallel where the first Atomic Bomb was tested and detonated. JFK was buried at the 33rd parallel. 33 is one of the 3 master numbers in numerology. The number of the Pagan God of Freemasonry is 33. Thirty-Three also represents .33 or 1/3 of the world's population and 1/3 of the angels cast out of heaven, as referenced in The Book of Revelations. Hillary deleted 33,000 emails. There are 33 amendments that have been added to the US Constitution, and in 1933 all of our Gold was removed from all 12 branches of the Federal Reserve Banks, and every man, woman and child and (its) assets became collateral against the U.S. dollar as Corporate Property.

"It is an established fact that the United States Federal Government has been dissolved by the Emergency banking Act [Social Security Act], March 9, 1933, 48 Stat. 1, Public Law 89-719; declared by President Roosevelt, being bankrupt and insolvent. H.J.R. 192, 73rd Congress in session, June 5, 1933. Joint Resolution to Suspend the Gold Standard and Abrogate. The Gold Clause dissolved the Sovereign Authority of the United States and the official capacities of all United States Governmental Offices, Officers, and Departments, and is further evidence that the United States Federal Government exists today in name only. United States Congressional Record, March 17, 1933 Vol.33."

- Rep. James Traficant, Jr. (Ohio) Addressing the House

Since the 'History of the Deep State' was published there has been an overwhelmingly positive response from readers about how thorough and detailed it was in explaining exactly what the Deep State is, and how it found its way into America. Unfortunately, one book is not enough to explain the vastness of the 'World Wide Web' the Deep State has spun and networked on a global scale.

Aside from the obvious and blatant political bias against my books, the only true criticisms were from some who had minor disagreements about exactly when the Deep State began. There are people who will argue the Deep State are merely an army of Bureaucrats and Obama holdovers. Some have debated it started in 1991 with George H.W. Bush, and the advent of the New World Order or that it began in 1927 with the formation of the C.I.A. There are also those who still believe it started with a foreign controlled banking system sometime between 1776 through 1781. The answer is quite simply that all of these hypotheses are technically correct, but unless we look at the big picture throughout history, we will never be able to grasp it completely.

One could also legitimately argue that the Deep State under Obama shadowed the same vein as Franklin Delano Roosevelt, who also almost nearly destroyed America, but was also incorrectly caricatured to this day as one of the greatest Presidents in U.S. history. History has a tough time remembering FDR was a Quasi-Socialist Democrat, a 33rd degree Freemason, a high-level Illuminatus who by force had the U.S. military going door to door throughout the U.S. seizing Americans gold (Executive Order 6101, demanding it back as U.S. property), partaking in the fomentation of World War II, and put The New Deal and its corresponding laws into place which partially dissolved the

U.S. Government, severing it in two; making it a Corporation or 'Cooperate Deep State' and a 'Nation State' divided against itself.

It is no wonder Obama fancied himself as FDR-like since the parallels between Obama and Roosevelt are strikingly similar:

Under Senator Barack Hussein Obama's Bill, [SB2433], the Poverty Act of 2007, United Nations military forces are permitted on American soil to confiscate weapons from United States citizens!

Barack Hussein Obama's place in history as a known Muslim, Marxist/ Socialist, and Divider-in-Chief was also whitewashed from Mainstream Media and history books; and replaced with a similar FDR-like caricature of a Christian, peacemaker, and unifier.

Before diving deeper into the number 33 and the evil it has caused this country, it's important to remember that today, over 50% of Americans believe there is a Deep State.

This demographic includes Republicans, Democrats, Libertarians, Independents, and a growing number of people in the United States, (before the Era of Trump) who after knowing the history of corruption in 'Government' would prefer to have nothing more to do with politics whatsoever.

However, among all of these vastly different Ideologically driven groups, how a Deep State is conceptualized for them is dramatically different. Republicans tend to visualize a cult-like elite people dressed in sackcloth, gathered around a Satanic circle, around a great Pagan statue in the dark of night, performing pedophiliac, occultist rituals and human sacrifice; praying for answers on new ways to trick low-class deplorables out of their hard-earned money. Democrats on the other hand, visualize the top 1% of the world's heartless and greedy Jew billionaires, wearing overpriced Armani suits, smoking cigars at the top floor of the Empire State Building, plotting the next big heist or money grab that they can capitalize on to cheat the middle-class and kill off every last poverty-stricken American.

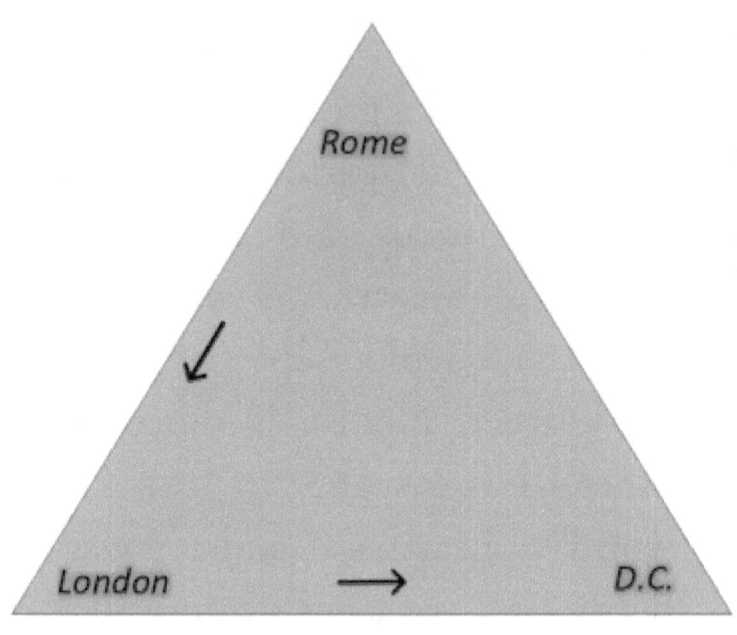

Although both of these conceptualizations are somewhat overblown and misleading both concepts form a hybrid amalgamation of a very real and stark vision of a Deep State, where at the top of the food chain of the Illuminati pyramid, Triad or 'Triangular Hierarchy' lies supremely at the Vatican in Rome, Italy. To better illustrate these complex web of Deep State triads ('Triads' because there are more than one; however, this is the oldest of all Deep State triads) we must map its points, as shown in the diagram above.

The Shining City on the Hill'

Before you jump out of your seat to say, this is going too far, how could Rome have any sway over politics, finance, media or anything in America?! – After reading this book you will have no doubts about the veracity of these claims.

This flowchart or mind map represents the oldest hierarchal structure of the flow of power from the top down in America. It is the 'Rosicrucian Triad', A.K.A. the 'Vatican triad' and it has served as the de facto model for later globalized power triads, which affect critical areas of the world of finance, religious instruction, Centralized banks, the International Monetary fund and what the Deep State considers the balancing of both opposing political parties, Democrat and Republican.

Incidentally, the Vatican is also a Central Bank and perhaps the most powerful of all Centralized Global Banks in the world. Which leads us to the topic of political party power structures in America. The Rosicrucian triad model is at least

242 years old and very likely predates our foundation and independence in 1776. The District of Columbia, of course, was not recognized as a city or Capital of the United States until July 6th, 1790. Prior to that day the location of what is now known as Washington D.C. was indeed intentionally built upon the city of Rome, Maryland!

The Washington Post correctly reported on October 7th, 1883, that there was a large estate (roughly 400 acres) in the area of what is now the southeast section of the Georgetown portion of the District of Columbia (D.C.). This estate was purchased by a man named Francis Pope on June 5th, 1663! Yes, he was a real person, his first name was Francis and his last name was Pope! Francis Pope was reported to have been 'fond of Italy' and named his farmland and city, 'Rome.' The adjacent small body of water to the south of 'Rome,' 'Goose Creek' was renamed Tiber, after the Tiber in Rome, Italy. Pope then boasted that America now had its very own Rome on the Tiber and that a Pope lived there!

This real-life story of Francis Pope is mind-blowing, and the account is not an old wives' tale or a rumor, it was thoroughly documented as a farmland purchase at the Annapolis, Maryland City Hall/Archives where it is cited in the next few pages for the skeptics of the world.

The account itself is particularly peculiar on many levels, most striking of all being that the man who formerly owned Washington D.C., not only had the last name Pope but that he had the first name, Francis. One can't help but wonder with the current liberal Francis, being Pope today; what the broader implications of this might suggest. Although there is always the possibility of a man with the last name Pope coincidently buying the land which is now our nation's capital in 1663, the circumstances that surround it, and what happens next makes the story that much more fantastical.

The Crown of England, The Vatican, The Illuminati, The Freemasons, and what I have coined 'The Brokers' were all involved in the forming of the foundation and layout of Washington D.C. and its purchase of this plot of land which was literally built upon the city of 'Rome'!

If you've already read History of the Deep State Volume I, you already know how much the Illuminati has carried the Roman tradition and its pagan practices into The Deep State's principles and practices. Ancient Bavarian and Bohemian culture has all come out of Rome, which they believe to be holy land. Its Pagan practices are still being used and carried out today, through the application of Communism/Socialism, Islamic

Sufism, and Hatha Yoga to topple Governments Globally and burrowed into the United States Government. Refer to Volume I for a complete description of its ancient, dark and long-plotting history.

Suffice it to say the original Roman Catholic's and the Jesuit Catholics have been at war for centuries, for some, and this fact might further complicate an already complicated situation which lies at the heart of the Vatican today. To complicate the situation more, Secret Societies inside Free Masonry and the Illuminati have also overthrown both sides of the Catholic-Jesuit plight. This will be further expounded upon in the chapter 'The Vatican Controls it all.'

That being said, Washington D.C. was deliberately built upon the city of

Rome, Maryland, not only for symbolic reasons but for the acquisition of power over the land which is regularly referred to as 'the shining city on the hill.' Where did this phraseology come from, and who coined it as such? In short, the Vatican-State Catholics did.

As explained in Volume I, everything The Deep State does is an inversion of God.

"Ye are the light of the world. A city that is set on an hill cannot be hid."
- Matthew 5:14

This single passage from the New Testament is from Jesus' Sermon on the mount, where the Deep State borrowed this phrase and have been overusing it out of context ever since. The meaning of this passage seems entirely symbolic, but predictably, for them, it has a literal sense.

For the Deep State, this hill is not symbolic at all, since Jesus gave his Sermon on a hill, they believe it means a holy hill somewhere on earth, and not just anywhere. The globalized elite has deemed Washington D.C. 'The Shining City on the Hill.' Why Washington D.C.? Well, because the District of Columbia is their 'New Jerusalem.'

"They will be back, because we remain, as difficult as we (D.C.) can be with each other, we remain that shining city on the hill, and they don't like it."

- James Comey

Further proof of this can be found by simply examining a map of D.C. and its surrounding area. Washington D.C. is purposefully situated at the top of the Potomac River (along a canal-like river, or vaginal opening). You can't make this stuff up. The map on the next page fully explains what is already in plain sight for anyone with eyes to see it. Virginia, due south of D.C., is exactly what it sounds like with the English root word 'Virgin.' The State of Maryland, just north of Washington D.C. is also exactly what it sounds like with the English root word 'Mary.' This, of course, puts our Nation's capital right in the middle of one colossal vagina, or in the wound of the Virgin Mary! The Virgin Mary, of course, is how the Roman Catholic Church identifies Jesus' mother, who bore the Son of God. All of this time we thought Jesus was born in Nazareth, yet according to the Deep State elites he was born right here in America, the New Jerusalem!

The three images seen here are more examples of 33 hidden in plain sight. The multiple uses of triangles form stars then finally a Great Pyramid, if you will, laid out with all of their corresponding lay lines, with their respective Ancient Egyptian degrees, Polygram's, pentagons and length using the numbers 6,9,33, and 377. All of these numbers are taken directly from the Great Pyramid of Egypt and are exact, down to the 6th degree axis from the king's chamber of the pyramid to the top of it, corresponding precisely to the distance of the White House to the Washington Monument, 377 feet (Six degrees north by northeast from its true north or middle axis).

"And here is the mind which hath wisdom. The seven heads are seven mountains, on which the woman sitteth."

- Revelation 17:9

Washington D.C. does not only follow the Roman model in its approach to the 'Common Law' legal system, it also mirrors its architecture, buildings, Pagan traditions, culture, bloodline, and occult practices.

More specifically, the Vatican, like D.C., is also a city-state encapsulated inside a larger Capital City (Rome), encapsulated inside of a larger Nation; Italy.

Rome has seven hills by nature, but D.C. also has seven hills, not by nature, but by design:

Seven Hills of Rome:

I. Capitoline Hill
II. Caelian Hill
III. Aventine Hill
IV. Esquiline Hill
V. Palatine Hill
VI. Quirinal Hill
VII. Viminal Hill

Seven Hills of D.C.:

I. Capitol Hill
II. Meridian Hill
III. Floral Hills
IV. Forest Hills
V. Hillbrook
VI. Hillcrest
VII. Knox Hill

The Catholic Encyclopedia's definition of the word 'Vatican', as it relates to its Vatican City identically describes its land and Deep State swampy district of 'ill-repute' with a shocking similarity to that of Washington D.C.'s 'swamp':

"The territory on the right bank of the Tiber between Monte Mario and Gianicolo (Janiculum) was known to antiquity as the <u>Ager Vaticanus, and, owing to its marshy character, the low-lying portion of this district enjoyed an ill-repute.</u> The origin of the name Vaticanus is uncertain; some claim that the name comes from a vanished Etruscan town called Viaticum."

The Etruscan's are a now extinct nationality who pre-date the Ancient Greco-Romans (Ancient Greece). *"No. 7.*

Francis Pope, owner of Rome, Maryland on the Tyber, June 5, 1663.

In the early records of Annapolis, one finds:

Francis Pope, transported since 1635; wife 1649. And in the Proceedings of the early

Assemblies:

Francis Pope—-member of the Assembly in September 1642 (2), and 1667 and 1670, he was Justice of the Peace for Charles County, Maryland. (3) In an old volume of precious records at Annapolis, Liber 6, folio 318:"June 5th, 1663, Lyd out for Francis Pope of this Province, Gent., a parcel of land in Charles County called Rome, lying on the East side of the Anacostian River (4) [meaning here, the main channel of the Potomac], beginning at a marked oak standing by the River side, the bounded tree of Captain Robert Troop and running north by the river for breadth the length 200 perches to a bounded oak standing at the mought of a bay or inlet called Tiber, bounding on the north by the said Lett and a line drawn east for the length of 320 perches to a bounded oak standing in the woods on the East with a line drawn south from the end of the former line until you meet with the exterior bounded tree of Robert Troop called

Scotland Yard on the south with the said land, on the west with the said river (Tyber), containing and now laid out for 400 acres more or less." Capt. Robert Troop's "Scotland Yard," itself north of the tract "New Troy" which extended far north of the Capitol (5) and Congressional Library of today, was therefore the southern boundary of Mr. Pope's Rome.

Yet, about 150 years later, in 1804, Tom Moore, the poet, 25 years of age, spent "near a week" with Mr. and Mrs. Merry[also with my great Aunt Marcia Burnes Van Ness—BP], the family of the early English minister, in Washington. Later, in a note to his Epistle to Thomas Hume, Moore gave his ideas of the infant city, and then wrote the following rhyme on the Capitol City of that date. "In fancy, now, beneath the twilight gloom, Come, let me lead thee o'er the second Rome. Where tribunes rule, where dusky David bow, And what was Goose creek once is Tiber now; This embryo Capital, where fancy sees

Squares in morasses, obelisks in trees

Which second-sighted seers, even now adorn

With shrines unbuilt and heroes yet unborn."

*David is David Burnes, my great Uncle, the father of Marcia Burnes Van Ness—BP

Moore writes of the Capital, not the Capitol !Perhaps he had never heard of Francis Pope, for certainly he would have mentioned "the Pope at Rome," or something to that effect in his verses. Yet, the popular interpretation has rolled on through the years, and many followers of the romantic now actually are convinced that Pope's "Rome" was on the site where our Nation's Capital Building now stands.

In the Manuscript Division of the Library of Congress, a set of original papers of the Bozeman family give interesting information regarding John Pope of "Rome," his wife Margaret, his brother Robert, and his daughter Frances. The will of John Pope, dated 1702, is given, as follows:

"I give and bequeath unto my loving brother Robert Pope, if living at my decease, the sum of 10 pounds sterling, to be paid by my executors within convenient time after my decease; but if my said brother should not then be living, my will is that my said executors pay the said sum of 10 Pounds sterling to the next heir of the said Robert Pope, and to him or her to hold and enjoy forever. Item. All the rest of my estate, both real and personal, I give and bequeath to my dear and loving wife, Margaret Pope, and to her heirs and assigns forever. But if it should so happen that my said wife marry or depart this life without any disposition of the said estate, then my will is that after my said wife's decease, <u>the same shall go and descend to my daughter Frances Ungle, and to the heir of her body begotten or to be begotten forever, and for want of said issue,</u>

then I give and bequeath the same estate to my aforesaid brother Robert Pope, near Bristol in the Kingdom of England, and to his heirs and as-signs forever, John Pope. There is a following notation made by C. N. Goldsborough in 1763 regarding the application of this will. It is noted that Margaret Pope never married again, but sold part of the real estate and mortgaged the rest. Goldsborough adds: "What estate had Mrs. Pope in the land called Rome under the will of her husband John Pope?" and "What estate had Mrs. Ungle in the land? She was Frances, the daughter of John Pope, mentioned in his will. Mrs. Pope had undoubtedly an estate in fee simple in the land called Rome under the will of her husband, etc."

Then follows the notation: "She (Mrs. Pope) sold her Lotts in Oxford to Mrs.

Ungle and the land called Rome she mortgaged, for 100 pounds Sterl. to be paid at the end of six years, without any express stipulation for interest; on the day of the signing of the mortgage an agreement signed by Mr. Grundy, the Mortgager, was made, expressing that Mrs. Grundy was to

have

Figure A: 18th Century drawing depicting 'The Shinning City on the

the use of the land six years and at the expiration of that time to restore it to Mrs. Pope. Whether the use of the land was for the interest of the money only, or for the Principal and interest, does not appear by any writing that has come to my hands. The original mortgage was found among Mrs. Ungle's papers, which shows that it had been given up by Mr. Grundy or my Mr. Lloyd his executor. Mrs. Pope never could have paid 100 pounds sterling. She borrowed it to enable her to go to England, in hopes of recovering her Eye sight, and was so needy after she returned that Mrs. Uncle chiefly supported her; I see by a letter from Mrs. Ungle to my father in 1722 that Mrs. Ungle had then thought of selling the land, so that it may reasonably be supposed that the mortgage to Mr. Grundy was discharged.

"Query: Is this act of Mrs. Pope's such a disposition as will defeat that part of John

Pope's will which limits it to his brother Robert Pope and his heirs?"

Further investigation might prove that John Pope, in Oxford Town, Talbot County, Maryland, was related to the original patentee of Rome, Francis Pope, who arrived in Maryland "since 1635," and that John Pope had named his only child, his daughter Frances, for her grandfather Francis Pope. If it be true that Francis Pope of Rome died and left his property to John Pope of Oxford, and that the "Rome" mentioned in the grant of 1663 to Francis Pope and in the will of 1702 of John Pope are the same place, then can we understand why the name "Rome" faded away from the area of the National Capital in so complete a manner, leaving only the romantic verses written later by Mr. Moore."

- From the Annapolis, Maryland City Hall/Archives, Oxford Town at the house of Mr. John Pope, 1693

POLITICAL PARTY TRIADS

"Corporations are privately owned businesses, meaning that the Corporate United States belongs to one or more private individuals, which is always governed by a Board of Directors. The Corporate United States is privately owned by a group of European Royal and Elite individuals tied to the Federal Reserve System and the letters of incorporation are recorded in the Vatican. The President of the United States is actually the CEO of the United States and the Congress and all others are corporate employees. Everything they do is in the interest of the corporate owners! I can't

access those documents because of National Security".

- *Retired US Judge Dale*

The topic of why America has been intentionally split into two diametrically opposed political parties brings us back to the number 33. The ever-prevalent letter 'G' in Free Masonry is from A to Z in the alphabet (26), then circling back again from to A to G is 33. Free Masons, of course designed the layout of Washington D.C., our Nation's Capital and the number 33 is the most important number of all numbers. Why? You might think 6 would be more important. Thirty-Three is built into the number 6. Three plus three is 6, and for those who think nine is more important in Numerology, that is also complete in this master Mason number; 3 X 3 is 9. But why is 33 so important? It is simply because .33 is 1/3 of the angles cast out of heaven – or the fallen angels which they place so much value in. Thirty-three is more sacred than 13 or any number associated with the occult. It represents heaven and hell, and the most extreme dualities in God and in nature. In fact, duality is there favorite mechanism because it is meant for one purpose only, to divide us.

"There is nothing which I dread so much as a division of the republic into two great parties, each arranged under its leader, and concerting measures in opposition to each other. This, in my humble apprehension, is to be dreaded as the greatest political evil under our Constitution."

- John Adams

The symbol on the left part of the diagram is of the 'Rockefeller Triad', the 'Socialist/Left-wing faction of the Deep State' or more commonly known as 'The Trilateral Commission' As you can see all three of its cities, Tokyo, Paris, and Washington D.C. and their corresponding Globalized Central Banks, depicted here working synergistically towards the middle forming a triangle, diamond, and pyramid. The Deep state has been consistent its use of the two colors black and white, symbolizing the duality of nature, Yin and Yang (right of the Trilateral Commission's moniker), Good and Evil, God and Devil, Man and Woman, or in this case, the Liberal and Conservative duality of American politics. More specifically, the Socialist and Communist elements of the left opposing the right. It is widely believed that Socialism began with Carl Marx, it did not; It began in China and its eastern counterparts in Japan and France. The idea of a Socialist State isn't new at all. its philosophy is ancient, especially in Asia and more recently in the 1700s during the 'enlightenment period' by a French Illuminist and the father of modern Socialism, Jean-Jacques Rousseau. In fact, Rousseau has eluded historians on the right side of politics, but the left knows exactly who he was, and to this day hold his writings in great reverence. Without going into the breadth of his work, he essentially held the idea that man's nature was evil and that we ought to be forced as societies and nations to live more as the Native Americans did. Carl Marx and Adam Weishaupt especially expanded on this philosophy and weaponized it in the application of quickly destroying Nations from within. Jean-Jacques often wrote about the idea of the wastefulness of work in achieving one's goals and the concept of happiness was just that, a concept that was unattainable within a Capitalistic system.

The Bill of Rights also has hidden duality intentionally built into it, when examining the use of the phrase 'life, liberty and the pursuit of happiness'. Most of us incorrectly attribute the phrase to have originated directly from the document itself. It does not however, the original application of this phrase was used by John Locke in 1689 minus the 'pursuit of happiness'; in 'A Letter Concerning Toleration', where Locke uses, "Life, liberty, and the possession of outward things." As can clearly be seen, Thomas Jefferson (33rd degree Master Mason and Illuminatus) borrowed the beginning of this timeless phrase from John Lock (a Capitalist). The second half of the phrase, 'pursuit of happiness' was borrowed from the teachings of Jean-Jacques Rousseau (a Socialist), who believed happiness was only attainable for the elite, unless what he described as "instances where particular ends or goals individuals happen to converge, so that they gain from cooperating with one another in the pursuit of something that will bring satisfaction [not capital] to them all." Rousseau's 'pursuit of happiness' as he describes it, is the very definition of Socialism. The literal meaning of the phrase life, 'liberty and the pursuit of happiness doesn't change', but as a rule, inserting encoded duality in plain sight is how Free Masons, the Illuminati, and the Deep State have always operated and continue to do so to this day!

Again, going back to the two warring triads, the Rosicrucian and Rockefeller; both systems oppose each other politically, but also work together synergistically.

George Washington, however was seemingly unaware of these dualities at work in our political system, most likely because Jefferson was working in large part independently, when drafting the Declaration of Independence and Constitution, the only part the other parties contributed in writing it was in its redrafting. Proof that Washington opposed dichotomy or duality in

American Government anywhere and especially in a divided Political-Party system is clear because he warned about its very real consequences for the future and that this inherent duality in America might eventually destroy us as a country:

"The alternate domination of one faction over another, sharpened by the spirit of revenge, natural to party dissension, which in different ages and countries has perpetrated the most horrid enormities, is itself a frightful despotism. But this leads at length to a more formal and permanent despotism. The disorders and miseries, which result, gradually incline the minds of men to seek security and repose in the absolute power of an individual; and sooner or later the chief of some prevailing faction, more able or more fortunate than his competitors, turns this disposition to the purposes of his own elevation, on the ruins of Public Liberty

Without looking forward to an extremity of this kind, (which nevertheless ought not to be entirely out of sight), the common and continual mischiefs of the spirit of party are sufficient to make it the interest and duty of a wise people to discourage and restrain it.

It serves always to distract the Public Councils, and enfeeble the Public Administration. It agitates the Community with ill-founded jealousies and false alarms; kindles the animosity of one part against another, foments occasionally riot and insurrection. It opens the door to foreign influence and corruption, which find a facilitated access to the government itself through the channels of party passions. Thus, the policy and the will of one country are subjected to the policy and will of another.

There is an opinion, that parties in free countries are useful checks upon the administration of the Government, and serve to keep alive the spirit of Liberty. This within certain limits is probably true; and in Governments of a Monarchical cast, Patriotism may look with indulgence, if not with favor, upon the spirit of party. But in those of the popular character, in Governments purely elective, it is a spirit not to be encouraged. From their natural tendency, it is certain there will always be enough of that spirit for every salutary purpose. And, there being constant danger of excess, the effort ought to be, by force of public opinion, to mitigate and assuage it. A fire not to be quenched, it demands a uniform vigilance to prevent its bursting into a flame, lest, instead of warming, it should consume."

As prophetic as Washington's dire warning for America was in the 18th century, the idea of destroying our nation by dividing us has been planned and contrived by the Deep State from day one for America; like everything else they do, the psychological tactics and warfare applied against the 'State' rarely go wrong, that is until Trump became President. But is it possible to undo 242 years of American Duality now deeply rooted in the fabric of our political culture? Even if the two-party system were amended from the Constitution into a one-party system, we are still left with 12 generations of people completely polarized in their thinking and political leanings. Since most of the public is viewed as sheeple by the Deep State, cause and effect wouldn't bring this to pass alone. What we are witnessing on a daily basis since President Trump has taken office is nothing short of Deep State mob hypnosis and mind control aimed at the American people.

Here is where an explanation of the Political Triads that now govern the world is necessary to see the bigger picture of this now globalized high stakes game of division took shape in America. The aforementioned Vatican-London-D.C. Triad has already been cited in previous pages, this was the only known political model which has typically played both sides of our political system, until 1933 when a more organized, powerful and better-funded opposing family arrived in to completely dismantle our Constitution from every conceivable angle. It started in 1913 to be more precise; but even 1913 had a decade's long build-up to what is still to this day, the greatest financial heist which has been perpetrated on our country.

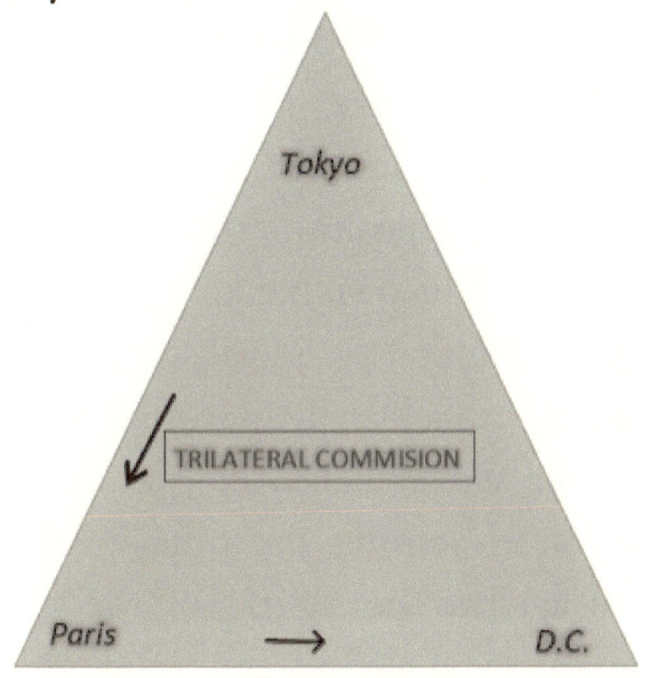

For now, we will call the Vatican-London-Triad system of centralized power the 'Rosicrucian Triad' which now is attempting to play its traditional role as working for the right-wing of the Deep State. Before the turn of the 19th century the role of the 'Rosicrucian Triad' was simply to keep control over both political parties and the manipulation of Banking through our Centralized banks. Everything changed when the Rockefeller family came as a controlled opposition to the Rothchild family with its own bankers and financial brokers with a Socialist/Communist agenda with a little help from China, and all three World War 2 axis powers slowly but surely joining the official left-wing triad against the right! For the skeptics who may be saying this is verging on conspiratorial, the proof is in the fact that the Rockefeller family fully funded World War I and II, and by 1973, the Trilateral Commission was formed as a corporation owned by the Rockefellers under President Jimmy Carter. This should put any naysayers' arguments to rest, since it is in plain sight:

"One-sixth of the total wealth of the world was represented by members of the Jekyll Island Club."

-New York Times on May 3, 1931, on George Baker, J.P. Morgan's associate.

Beginning in 1913 the big banking families of Jekyll Island took all the gold from their Federal Reserve Banks (it was never ours, being foreign internationally owned), robbing us blind and demanding full payment, which of course we as a Nation could not pay because our Gold somehow came up missing! The bankers demanded their debts be repaid somehow, but were kind enough to allow us to run on their extended credit, until we figured out a way to repay our long-time debt masters.

The dark years that followed this experiment was also planned decades in advance, since money backed by no Gold or commodity would eventually be found out and terrify the American people, which it did almost immediately the banking panic of 1913, when rumors spread about a meeting of the most well know big bankers like J.P. Morgan at Jekyll Island had secretly plotted making the U.S. dollar worthless. Many Americans pulled their money out of the banks simultaneously, but this was short-lived, and confidence was quickly restored. Nevertheless, by 1929 America had its first massive Stock market crash and *by October of that same year the illusion of our dollar having any inherent value vanished from every Americans mind, and the big lie had run its course; causing millions of people to take their money and gold out of the bank and run for the hills to hoard what little they had left of any monetary value.*

By 1933, The Deep State Bankers who were celebrating the power of their sacred 33 and what it represented, knew America was poised to sell their soul now, and the Deep State had the perfect solution; to suspend the U.S. Constitution on a basis of a technically putting it in a perpetual state of Emergency (The Emergency Act) to make every man, woman, and child and its assets the new collateral against the U.S. dollar and to make America a Corporation; trademarking it as U.S.A. INC:

United States Congressional Record March 17, 1993 Vol. 33, page H-1303:

Speaker-Rep. James Traficant, Jr. (Ohio) Addressing the House: "Mr. Speaker, we are here now in chapter 11. Members of Congress are official trustees presiding over the greatest reorganization of any Bankrupt entity in world history, the U.S. Government. We are setting forth hopefully, a blueprint for our future. There are some who say it is a coroner's report that will lead to our demise. It is an established fact that the United States Federal Government has been dissolved by the Emergency Banking Act, March 9, 1933, 48 Stat. 1, Public Law 89-719; declared by President Roosevelt, being bankrupt and insolvent. H.J.R. 192, 73rd Congress m session June 5, 1933 - Joint

Resolution To Suspend The Gold Standard and Abrogate The Gold Clause dissolved the Sovereign Authority of the United States and the official capacities of all United States Governmental Offices, Officers, and Departments and is further evidence that the United States Federal Government exists today in name only. The receivers of the United States Bankruptcy are the International Bankers, via the United Nations, the World Bank and the International Monetary Fund. ALL United States Offices, Officials, and Departments are now operating within a de facto status in name only under Emergency War Powers. With the Constitutional Republican form of Government now dissolved, the receivers of the Bankruptcy have adopted a new form of government for the United

States. This new form of government is known as a Democracy, being an established Socialist/Communist order under a new governor for America. This act was instituted and established by transferring and/or placing the Office of the Secretary of Treasury to that of the Governor of the International Monetary Fund. Public Law 94-564, page 8, Section H.R. 13955 reads in part: "The U.S. Secretary of Treasury receives no compensation for representing the United States." Gold and silver were such a powerful money during the founding of the united states of America, that the founding fathers declared that only gold or silver coins can be "money" in America. Since gold and silver coinage were heavy and inconvenient for a lot of transactions, they were stored in banks and a claim check was issued as a money substitute. People traded their coupons as money, or "currency." Currency is not money, but a money substitute. Redeemable currency must promise to pay a dollar equivalent in gold or silver money. Federal Reserve Notes (FRNs) make no such promises, and are not "money." A Federal Reserve Note is a debt obligation of the federal United States government, NOT "money." The federal United States government and the U.S. Congress were not and have never been authorized by the Constitution for the united states of America to issue currency of any kind, but only lawful money, gold and silver coin. It is essential that we comprehend the distinction between real money and paper money substitute. One cannot get rich by accumulating money substitutes;

one can only get deeper into debt. We the People no longer have any "money." Most Americans have not been paid any "money" for a very long time, perhaps not in their entire life. Now do you comprehend why you feel broke? Now, do you understand why you are "bankrupt," along with the rest of the country? Federal Reserve Notes (FRNs) are unsigned checks written on a closed account. FRNs are an inflatable paper system designed to create debt through inflation (devaluation of currency). whenever there is an increase of the supply of a money substitute in the economy without a corresponding increase in the gold and silver backing, inflation occurs. Inflation is an invisible form of taxation that irresponsible governments inflict on their citizens. The

Federal Reserve Bank who controls the supply and movement of FRNs has everybody fooled. They have access to an unlimited supply of FRNs, paying only for the printing costs of what they need. FRNs are nothing more than promissory notes for U.S. Treasury securities (T-Bills) - a promise to pay the debt to the Federal Reserve Bank. There is a fundamental difference between "paying" and "discharging" a debt. To pay a debt, you must pay with value or substance (i.e. gold, silver, barter or a commodity). With FRNs, you can only discharge a debt. You cannot pay a debt with a debt currency system. You cannot service a debt with a currency that has no backing in value or substance. No contract in Common law is valid unless it involves an exchange of "good & valuable consideration."

Unpayable debt transfers power and control to the sovereign power structure that has no interest in money, law, equity or justice because they have so much wealth already. Their lust is for power and control. Since the inception of central banking, they have controlled the fates of nations. The Federal Reserve System is based on the Canon law and the principles of sovereignty protected in the Constitution and the Bill of Rights. In fact, the international bankers used a "Canon Law Trust" as their model, adding stock and naming it a "Joint Stock Trust." The U.S. Congress had passed a law making it illegal for any legal "person" to duplicate a "Joint Stock Trust" in 1873. The Federal Reserve Act was legislated post-facto (to 1870), although post facto laws are strictly forbidden by the

Constitution. [1:9:3] The Federal Reserve System is a sovereign power structure separate and distinct from the federal United States government. The Federal Reserve is a maritime lender, and/or maritime insurance underwriter to the federal United States operating exclusively under Admiralty/Maritime law. The lender or underwriter bears the risks, and the Maritime law compelling specific performance in paying the interest, or premiums are the same. Assets of the debtor can also be hypothecated (to pledge something as a security without taking possession of it.) as security by the lender or underwriter. The Federal Reserve Act stipulated that the interest on the debt was to be paid in gold. There was no stipulation in the Federal Reserve Act for ever paying the principle. Prior to 1913, most Americans owned clear, allodial title to property, free and clear of any liens or mortgages until the Federal Reserve Act (1913) "Hypothecated" all property within the federal United States to the Board of Governors of the Federal Reserve, in which the Trustees (stockholders) held legal title. The U.S. citizen (tenant, franchisee) was registered as a "beneficiary" of the trust via his/her birth certificate. In 1933, the federal United States hypothecated ALL of the present and FUTURE PROPERTIES, assets and labor of their SUBJECTS," the 14th Amendment U.S. citizen, to the Federal Reserve System. In return, the Federal Reserve System agreed to extend the federal United States corporation all the credit "money substitute" it needed. Like any other debtor, the federal United

States government had to assign collateral and security to their creditors as a condition of the loan. Since the federal United States didn't have any assets, they assigned the private property of their "economic slaves", the U.S. citizens as collateral against the unpayable federal debt. They also pledged the unincorporated federal territories, national parks forests, birth certificates, and nonprofit organizations, as collateral against the federal debt. All has already been transferred as payment to the international bankers. Unwittingly, America has returned to its pre-American Revolution, feudal roots whereby all land is held by a sovereign and the common people had no rights to hold allodial title to property. Once again, We the People are the tenants and sharecroppers renting our own property from a Sovereign in the guise of the Federal Reserve Bank. We the people have exchanged one master for another. This has been going on for over eighty years without the "informed knowledge" of the American people, without a voice protesting loud enough. Now it's easy to grasp why America is fundamentally bankrupt. Why don't more people own their properties outright? Why are 90% of Americans mortgaged to the hilt and have little or no assets after all debts and liabilities have been paid? Why does it feel like you are working harder and harder and getting less and less? We are reaping what has been sown, and the results of our harvest is a painful bankruptcy, and a foreclosure on American property, precious liberties, and a way of life. Few of our elected representatives in Washington, D.C. have dared to tell the truth. The federal United States is bankrupt. Our children will inherit this unpayable debt, and the tyranny to enforce paying it. America has become completely bankrupt in world leadership, financial credit and its reputation for courage, vision and human rights. This is an undeclared economic war, bankruptcy, and economic slavery of the most corrupt order! Wake up America! Take back your Country."

Since 1933 with the help of the father of American Socialism, Franklin Delano Roosevelt extending into the Carter Administration through present day, the Deep State has reenacted the Emergencies Act (the Quasi-State of Martial law) suspending the U.S. Constitution in theory, although for some it is already a reality. However, since we are still a Republic being governed by the laws of the U.S. Constitution this theory is still in flux; depending on which political party is in power: its Representative Presidents, Senators, Congressmen, and Supreme Court Justices all rely on this power struggle over U.N. International law VS U.S. Constitutional law. Since the advent of the New World Order's beginning in 1991 all Presidents through 2017 including: Bush Sr., Bill Clinton, George W. Bush and Obama were 'NEW WORLD ORDER', the ringleader being George Herbert Walker Bush. The idea being that a New World Order is to have a centralized and Globalized One-World Government (The United Nations through the direction of the U.S. President) and that U.N. globalized/

International law will eventually wholly take precedence over the United States Constitution.

"Not only were many of the founders of the United States government Masons, but they received aid from a secret and august body existing in Europe which helped them to establish this country for a peculiar and particular purpose known only to the initiated few."

—Manly P Hall 33rd degree Mason. 'The Secret Teachings of All Ages', 1928

Free Masonry has always been divided into two. The Egyptian Rite and the Scottish Rite, as have been the Illuminati and the World Banking Triad families (Rockefeller and Rothchild). This division has occurred over decades and now centuries before the advent of the New World Order. Why should the New

World Order suddenly become one, and not DIVIDED?! That is its stated mission, 'oneness'. However, the founders of all these groups created a twisted experiment of a 1/3 division (33) that it is not just interlocking but is now woven so tightly that there are divisions divided at 3 degrees of secrecy; the idea behind these divided groups is that they must either become one or destroy themselves. Either way with this system in place, the American people and the world loses.

"There is no salvation for civilization, or even the human race, other than the creation of a world government."
—*Albert Einstein*

"It is dangerous to be right when the government is wrong."
—*Voltaire (1694 - 1778)*

"...the New Atlantis sets forth an ideal government of the earth. It foretells that day when in the midst of men there shall rise up a vast institution composed of the philosophic elect—an order of illumined men banded together for the purpose of investigating the laws of life and the mysteries of the universe ... The age of boundaries is closing, and we are approaching a nobler era when nations shall be no more; when the lines of race and caste shall be wiped out; when the whole earth shall be under one order, one government, one administrative body."

—-Manly P. Hall "Lectures on Ancient Philosophy, 1970

"Countless people will hate the New World Order and will die protesting against it."

—*H.G. Wells, The New World Order, 1939*

"*In Germany, they came first for the Communists, and I didn't speak up because I wasn't a Communist. Then they came for the Jews, and I didn't speak up because I wasn't a Jew. Then they came for the trade unionists, and I didn't speak up because I wasn't a trade unionist. Then they came for the Catholics, and I didn't speak up because I was a Protestant. Then they came for me, and by that time no one was left to speak up.*"

—*Martin Niemueller*

"*We are very largely divided in our convictions about the realities of things; and unless something is done to overcome this division, we will never be able to cooperate in a New World Order of thinking. The time has come that we have got to either find a spiritual value in our own nature, and do something about it; or we are never going to be able to fill this New World, that we so gravely hope to find."*

—-Manly P. Hall

Skull & Bones

"Barbara Walters: Are you a Christian?

"George H.W. Bush: If by being a Christian, you ask if I am 'Born Again,' then yes, I am a Christian."

Our world has been inundated and usurped by secret societies by the thousands. Many of these Societies are veiled under the cloak of another such as the Illuminati hidden under the veil of Freemasonry; then hiding itself into another more venerable institution, such as the Vatican or a Trilateral . This three-layered approach to hiding a Societies true identity is commonly referred to as the 'Three degrees of Secrecy.' Instead of the third layer being the Vatican for instance, it could be a bank, religious institution, business, corporation, political party, a or even a global triad power structure.

Since there are so many different groups with their corresponding degrees of secrecy, classifying them is of course shrouded in secrecy and therefore too vast and numerous to list. However, we can begin with three Societies which are commonly known today, which are the CFR (Council on Foreign Relations), The Bilderberg Group, and Skull and Bones. We have already discussed the CFR in Volume one as it relates to the World Court and the State Department with its Socialist/Communist ties going as far back as the early 1920s via the Rockefeller Foundation in America. The Bilderberg Group, and how it relates to these other Groups/Societies will be discussed at length in a later chapter. This leads us now, to the core of this encapsulated three degrees of secrecy, Skull and Bones.

Skull and Bones was founded in 1832 by an American business Mogul, William Huntington Russell. Russell formed the secret society with Alphonso Taft (U.S. President William Taft's father). Alphonso Taft later became elevated to various high-ranking posts in Federal Government; Secretary of War, Attorney General, Ambassador to Russia and Ambassador to Austria. William Huntington Russell owned the Corporate name for Skull and Bones, 'Russell & Company Trust,' a transport company which cornered the opium market and smuggled it into China during 'the opium wars.' He also later served on the Board of Visitors in 1863, and many believe he was responsible for single-handedly fomenting the advent of the Civil War as an occultist and money-making endeavor for the benefit of himself and his elite banking constituents.

Russell was also active in politics being a 'Whig' from 1845 through 1847 then becoming one of the prominent members responsible for the formation of what is now the 'Republican Party.' He was most notably recognized however for his work at Yale, being a teacher, scholar, psychologist and occultist hypnotist, learning the dark arts of Bavarian Illuminati occultist Black Magic during his elusive six-year hiatus to Bavaria, Germany. After returning from Bavaria, armed with the Illuminati teachings of Weishaupt's 'Order of the Illuminati,' he then brought everything he had learned back to Yale, with the help of family ties to Noadiah Russell who co-founded the College in 1701.

The name Skull and Bones originates from the hanging ornament that was displayed at the societies entrance door, which was of skull and crossbones. The Skull and Bones society is also known as the 'Order of Death,' 'Corporation Skull,' but it is now just referred to as simply, 'The Order.'

Upon returning from Bavaria, during his senior year At Yale, William Huntington Russell officially created the fraternal Society 'Skull and Bones'. Three-Twenty-two (322) is often associated with the code of the 'Brotherhood of Death' being established and founded officially in 1832. Although the 32 relates to the year of its foundation in 1832 it is also symbolic of 3 or one-third, .333 being divided into 2 given us the Satanic number .666. The second 2 in 322 spells out its formation of the 2nd international order. Skull and Bones was an extension and enhancement of the 1st international Order being the 'Order of the Illuminati.' This 2nd Order was also 'international' in scope because both orders were already global by 1776. As explained in Volume one, the 'Order of the Illuminati,' established by the former Jesuit priest and lawyer (also out of Bavaria, Germany) Adam Weishaupt in 1776; the teachings of the Illuminati spread like wildfire into the temples and lodges of the Freemasons across Europe and around the world. These Freemasonic lodgings were already set up around the world, making it very easy to become 'international' and global in scope. 'Skull & Bones' was the 2nd International, Globalized Order, and the 3rd International Order is 'The New World Order' established in 1981 and launched into practice in 1991 by Bonesman, Bush Sr.

The Skull & Bones Initiation

Since 1833 (again, '33' is not a coincidence) every year only 15 juniors are "tapped," to be chosen for admission and membership into America's highest-ranking Secret Society. Initiates are propositioned, after being tapped with the question, "Skull & Bones. Accept or reject?" Those who accept are invited to the Bones Temple to partake in the initiation ceremony. This tradition is known as 'Tap Day,' and it has become a private ceremony after 1953. There are also two other less well-known Yale Societies, which are the sister brotherhoods of Skull & Bones; Scroll & Key and Wolfs Head.

Before being Knighted into the 'Brotherhood of Death,' the Initiates then meet at Bones headquarters, 64 High St. or the 'Tomb.' The Tomb is a windowless building, which has a private helicopter landing pad. Yale's fraternal tradition has historically been that Juniors are to be brought into a yard where the Senior class of Knighted Bondsmen would encircle the Junior class choosing the initiates who are then invited into initiation. Since 1953 this tradition has changed and is now strictly private, in order to lessen the humiliation of Juniors who would be seen as being rejected from this establishments patriarchal ruling class.

Figure 3: Skull & Bones Fraternity house or 'The Tomb'

Initiation into Skull & Bones begins with its initiates being blindfolded while masturbating before the other members and taking an oath not to reveal their membership into Skull & Bones. The initiate is then required to recall and detail all of his previous sexual exploits, while lying naked in a coffin filled with blood, skulls and bones. They are then prompted to kiss the feet of the Senior class

Knights, then proceed to drink blood from a chalice before being fully inducted. The initiate is then unblindfolded and introduced to their future brothers of the Order. The Knights introduce themselves, adorned with masks covering their faces completely. The masks include those of the Knights of Malta, Don Quixote, the Devil, Uncle Tobyn and the Pope. The induction of the initiation into Bones ends with every Knight saluting the newly Knighted initiate with an extended hand hail Hitler salute.

The newly recruited initiates become 'Knights' and spend their senior year being indoctrinated with the secrets of 'Sex Magic' and similar occultist and Kabbalist teachings. After the Knighthood's teachings are complete, the newly crowned Bonesman become 'Patriarchs' and upon graduating Yale they will spend a lifetime as Patriarchal royalty, given all the special treatment as the original Bavarian and Roman Patriarchy. Over the course of their lifetime the Brotherhood of the Skull attend annual meetings at 'the Deer Hand Club' as Patriarchs and enjoy all the fringe benefits and financial support from the Russell Trust Association.

Ron Rosenbaum describes the Skull and Bones initiation as follows:

New man placed in coffin - carried into central part of building. New man chanted over and reborn into society. Removed from coffin and given robes with symbols on it. A bone with his name on it is tossed into bone heap at start of evening. Initiates plunged naked into mud pile.

"The senior societies are such peculiarly Yale institutions that it will be difficult for an outsider fully to appreciate their significance...Nothing like them exists elsewhere ...Harvard is the only college where, under similar conditions they possibly could exist."- Lyman Bagg, *Four Years at Yale*

Volume 1, Number 1, of The Iconoclast, October of 1873:

'We speak through a new publication, because the college press is closed to those who dare to openly mention 'Bones'.... Out of every class Skull and Bones takes its men. They have gone out into the world and have become, in many instances, leaders in society. They have obtained control of Yale. Its business is performed by them. Money paid to the college must pass into their hands, and be subject to their will. No doubt they are worthy men in themselves, but the many, whom they looked down upon while in college, cannot so far forget as to give money freely into their hands. Men in Wall Street complain that the college comes straight to them for help, instead of asking each graduate for his share. The reason is found in a remark made by one of Yale's and America's first men: 'Few will give but Bones men and they care far more for their society than they do for the college..Year by year the deadly evil is growing. The society was never as obnoxious to the college as it is today, and it is just this ill-feeling that shuts the pockets of non-members. Never before has it shown such arrogance and self-fancied superiority. It grasps the College Press and endeavors to rule it all. It does not deign to show its credentials, but clutches at power with the silence of conscious guilt. To tell the good which Yale College has done would be well-nigh impossible. To tell the good she might do would be yet more difficult. The question, then, is reduced to this - on the one hand lies a source of incalculable good - on the other a society guilty of serious and far-reaching crimes. It is Yale College against Skull and Bones!! We ask all men, as a question of right, which should be allowed to live?'

In case there is any doubt as to whether Skull and Bones, the Illuminati and The New World Order have any documented relationship to one another, the corresponding two statements have been highlighted to exemplify just how interlocked these groups are: "Bones is a chapter of corps of a German university. It should properly be called the Skull and Bones chapter. General Russell, its founder, was in Germany before his senior year and formed a warm friendship with a leading member of a German society. The meaning of the permanent number 322 in all Bones literature is that it was founded in '32 as the second chapter of the German society. But the Bonesman has a pleasing fiction that his fraternity is a descendant of an old Greek patriot society founded by Demosthenes, who died in 322 BC....on arched walls above the vault of the sacred room 322. The slogan appears above a painting of skulls surrounded by Masonic symbols, a picture said to be a gift of the German chapter. *Wer war der Thor, wer*

Weiser, Bettler oder Kaiser? Ob Arm, ob Reich, im Tode gleich,"
or "Who was the fool, who the wise man, beggar or king? Whether
poor or rich, all's the same in death."
    —*File and Claw*

"a skeleton is pointed out to him (the initiate), at the feet
of which are laid a crown and a sword. *He is asked 'whether that
is the skeleton of a king, nobleman or a beggar.'* As he cannot
decide, the president of the meeting says to him, 'The character
of being a man is the only one that is importance'".
    —*John Birch Society on the confiscated documentation of
then 1785 Bavarian-Banned Order of the Illuminati, 1967*

PROMINENT BONDSMEN in U.S. History
    William Howard Taft — Class of 1878
    Walter Camp — Class of 1880
    Lyman Spitzer — Class of 1935
    Potter Stewart — Class of 1937
    McGeorge Bundy — Class of 1940
    George Herbert W Bush — Class of 1948
    William F. Buckley Jr. — Class of 1950
    John F. Kerry — Class of 1966
    George W. Bush — Class of 1968
    Prominent Skull & Bones surnames:
    Rockefeller Bush
    Vanderbilt Perkins
    Whitney Phelps
    Bundy Taft
    Stimson Lovett
    Harriman Sloane

Pinchot Pillsbury
Goodyear Kellogg

Weyerhaeuser Jay

THE BUSH FAMILY, THE Nazis & Skull & Bones

Another Prominent Bonesman in American history was Prescott Sheldon Bush (class of 1917), the father of President George Herbert Walker Bush and the grandfather of George W Bush. Prescott Bush was the Vice President of the Union banking Corporation in 1930, and held a partnership with German steel Mogul, Fitz Thyson. The Nazi war effort was funded by two Corporations, I.G. Farben and J.D. Rockefeller's U.S. Standard Oil Company. Farben supplied explosives to the Nazis as a German Company, while U.S. Standard Oil fueled the Nazi German tanks, planes and energy supply. As you can see, the Illuminati played both sides of WWII, with the United States and Germany both being complicit in aiding the Axis Powers of the Nazi German Military Industrial Complex. Not only were these 'warring nations' Corporations involved, but both sides of the American political system were as well. Rockefeller's played for the left while the Bush's played for the right, with none other than Nazi Germany's original patron and money laundering organization, Union Banking Corporation. Truman had the Thyson/Bush criminal enterprise shut down and seized in October of1942 for violating the 'Trading with the Enemies Act' for its affiliation and business with Nazi Germany during World War II. Bush's sidekick Fritz Thyson later when on to publish the book 'I paid Hitler'; while Prescott Bush later became a prominent U.S. Senator without political backlash or mention of his affiliation with the Third Rieke, of course this was covered up due to the fact that Prescott was a protected ruling class Patriarch of 'The Brotherhood of the Skull.' The Hearings of McCormick Dixting Committee in November 1934 prove beyond any doubt that JP Morgan, The Remington family, the Dupont Family, and Prescott Bush were planning to assassinate Socialist Franklin Delano Roosevelt, overthrow the U.S. Government and turn the United States Government into a Nazi Communist/Fascist State.

Controlling Both Sides & The New world order

In 2004 two of Americas foremost Patriarchs of the 'Brotherhood of Death' ran against each other; the 'Texan', George W. Bush, and John Kerry, a Democrat Bonesman from Massachusetts.

Graduating from Yale just two years from each other, Kerry in 1966, and Bush in 1968; America began to sense that there was something far too coincidental in two Yale University Bondsmen running for the highest office in the free world at the same time could only mean an elite ruling class Patriarchy were the unelected rulers of our world.

Whether the public would notice this strange coincidence or not made no difference to the Deep State. Moreover, and more importantly, how could two men who were indoctrinated from the same Secret Society, with the same Illuminati and Occultist background run against one another as two seemingly opposing political ideologies, unless they were working for a 'higher purpose' (a phrase used very often by the Deep State) and a new system of Governance? The New World Order was beginning to make sense.

To better grasp the beginnings of this dichotomy of the same one-world system of governance acting as two opposing systems, let's begin by examining the writings that were intercepted by the Bavarian authorities who banished the Illuminati found in the original publication of 'Order & Sect of the Illuminati:

"By this plan, we shall direct all mankind in this manner. And, by the simplest means, we shall set all in motion and in flames. The occupations must be so allotted and contrived that we may, in secret, influence all political transactions."

- Adam Weishaupt

The Presidents from 41 to 44 were not just of the 1st or 2nd Order anymore, instead; George Herbert Walker Bush, Bill Clinton, George W. Bush and Barrack Hussein Obama were all members of the New World Order; and all four of them worked for the same man, the ringleader, founder, and puppet master of the New World Order, Bush 41. George Herbert Walker Bush's father, Prescott Bush openly claimed to be responsible for inserting Richard Nixon into the Oval Office in 1952, by making Nixon Ike's running mate. From Vice-Presidency to Presidency in 1969 was a simple transition. George H. W. Bush took daddy Bush's Nazi roots to the next level and joined when he formed an alliance in 1981 at Kennebunkport, Maine with George Wallace and Bill Clinton. George H. W. Bush went on to become the 41st President in 1989, Bill Clinton followed in 1993, George W. Bush in 2001, and Obama was also selected to join the New World Order of Deep State Presidents in 2008.

Although Barrack Hussein Obama did not graduate Yale as a Bonesman, he did graduate from Harvard, which also has its own Secret Society and patriarchy: *"The senior societies are such peculiarly Yale institutions that it will be difficult for an outsider fully to appreciate their significance. Nothing like them exists elsewhere, <u>Harvard is the only college where, under similar conditions they possibly could exist.</u>"*

- Lyman Bagg, 'Four Years at Yale'

The TrilateralISTS, Bilderbergers
&
Corporate socialism

"Since I entered politics, I have chiefly had men's views confided to me privately. Some of the biggest men in the United States, in the field of commerce and manufacture, are afraid of something. They know that there is a power somewhere so organized, so subtle, so watchful, so interlocked, so complete, so pervasive, that they better not speak above their breath when they speak in condemnation of it."

— *Woodrow Wilson*

Before getting into the technicalities of the development of the complex Interlocking of international groups that have formed in recent history, it is important to keep in mind that upon peering into these groups individually that they are also woven into an even more complex interlocking system that has been developing over centuries; first as secret societies, then into globalized 'groups', then power structures or Triads (centralized triangulated points of power). The reason this is key is because upon minimizing the Deep State into one area, as just 'The Bilderberg Group,' or the 'Trilateral Commission', CFR, etcetera, one will easily get lost in the details of the bigger lie. For example, many people will focus on our perverse banking system and immediately conclude that everything is about Kabbalist Jews. Another example of a gross and inaccurate generalization is that since most of the world's oil comes out of the middle east that Islamists must somehow be to blame, and at the core of the Deep State. However, when we take a step back and look at the entire web that has now been spun globally, things also become equally distorted as an interlock that is far too confusing, and that could only be rationalized as evil run rampant at every corner of our world. This too is part of the Deep States grand illusion.

The only way outside of these two divided ways of thinking, is to first understand The Deep State's roots, origin and history, then all of its major components singularly. Only then can we take a step back to peer into the Deep State for what it is, a vast, monolithic and globalized network of corruption - always shrouded in at least three degrees of secrecy.

In Volume I of History of the Deep State, there was an emphasis on Socialism, Bavaria, the Roman Empire and the Illuminati. Why? Because without this foundational knowledge, the smaller details of secrecy of what then become groups, like the Trilateral Commission and the Bilderberg Group begin to look as though they could very well be just a large conglomerate of greedy, foreign-globalists who are simply attempting to take it all for themselves. Although at face value this can appear to be true, the bigger picture is again lost in the matrix.

The understanding of a Deep State being a globalized matrix rings especially true when discussing the Trilateral Commission, the Bilderbergers, and the CFR as they relate to the U.S. Federal Reserve Banks and their interlock to the IMF (International Monetary Banking Fund) and its affiliate World Banks, and 'Global Elite Banksters.'

The Bilderberg Group

"For more than a century, ideological extremist at either end of the political spectrum have seized upon well-publicized incidents such as my encounter with Castro to attack the Rockefeller family for the inordinate influence they claim we wield over American political and economic institutions. <u>Some even believe we are part of a secret cabal working against the best interests of the United States, characterizing my family and me as 'internationalists' and of conspiring with others around the world to build a more integrated global political and economic structure - one world, if you will. If that's the charge, I stand guilty, and I am proud of it."</u>

- David Rockefeller, from his book, Memoirs.

The Bilderberg Group are simply the representatives of the 'World Court,' who are the owners of six of the twelve private and foreign-run branches of the U.S. Federal Reserve Banks. These six bankers account for the Cooperate/Socialist half of the twelve 'Fed' bankers in total (seven make up a quorum, or majority). These twelve bankers are then divided into two opposing and warring groups; who also vote on world affairs (Not at the Bilderberg meetings, where there is no voting). They also somehow manage to work in harmony and 'synergistically,' in spite of their apparent opposition to one another.' If it all sounds confusing, that's by Deep State design, not for lack of the authors ability to write pithy and complete explanations. To make matters worse, these Corporate/ Socialists, who make up five members of the World Court, are also representatives for their spokesman and founder of the Bilderberg Group, John Rockefeller (or 'the Rockefellers'). Here again, we have more degrees of secrecy, all interlocked, yet shrouded by at least five layers of secrecy, then divided in two;

adding a sixth degree of confusion to an already complex Deep State Matrix of secrecy.

The notion of holding private meetings with world leaders, moguls of business and finance, politicians and some of the world's most prominent and influential people in an effort to subtly influence United States economic policy, and political events across the Western Hemisphere and Western Europe is not new or exclusive to the Bilderberg Group. In fact, the same people who founded The Bilderberg group were also members of what was previously known as the notorious Bohemian Grove Club, established in 1872 by San Franciscans. Bohemian Grove also played a key role in shaping post-war politics, its policies, and political influence over the U.S. and the West a century before the formation of the Bilderberg group, according to an excerpt from an article entitled 'The Invisible Power House':

"It was at the Grove, it is said, that the Manhattan Project was set up and that Eisenhower was selected as the Republicans' candidate for 1952."

Yet, by the early fifties, elites in Europe and North America were becoming more interested in hosting private meetings for a more globalized world, inside the world of business, politics and finance, to discuss what was then called the 'Atlantic community' or 'Atlanteans' in order to 'create a better understanding of trends affecting Western nations,' on a far broader scale.

By May 29th, 1954 the first Bilderberg meeting was held, being fully organized, sponsored, and financed by the Rockefeller's via John Rockefeller and then CIA director, General Walter Bedel Smith. The first meeting was held under the chairmanship of Prince Bernhard of the Netherlands at the Hotel De Bilderberg in Oosterbeek, Holland; and ever since the meetings have been called Bilderberg meetings. According to Bilderberg's document of 1989: "That pioneering meeting grew out of the concern expressed by many leading citizens on both sides of the Atlantic that Western Europe and North America were not working together as closely as they should on matters of critical importance. It was felt that regular, off-the-record discussions would help create a better understanding of the complex forces and major trends affecting Western nations in the difficult post-war period."

The first Horary Chairman of the Bilderberg Club, Prince Bernard of the Netherlands, was also a former Nazi SS party member, and a former executive of the Nazi oil company IG Farben, who fueled the Nazi Germany army during World War 2. It is said that Prince Bernhard chose the invitees from the European countries to the first Bilderberg meeting, and C.D. Jackson was responsible for the Americans that were to attend.

Jackson, incidentally later went on to become President Eisenhower's {Boeheim Grove's (Bilderberg Group), unelected President}. assistant for psychological warfare.

Bilderbergers typically invite between one-hundred and-fifteen and one-hundred and fifty elite globalists to its meeting yearly. Since the Bilderberg Group was formed during the Cold War, it was built around the false premise of building up the west in an effort to fight the Communist threat from the U.S.S.R. and Soviets. Through the dismantling of the Soviet Union to present day, this has, of course not stopped the meetings from taking place; instead roughly ninety of its annual guests are from Western Europe and approximately 35 to 70 are from North America. Of these approximate 115 Socialist-minded guests, a third (.33) are chosen from the elite of Skull and Bonesman and or the 'New World Order' affiliated politicians of the World. The other two thirds (.666 by Deep State design) are chosen from commodities markets, education, corporate executive status and Main Stream Media.

The 'official' stated objectives, given by the Bilderberg Group was 'to bring together the leaders of business, finance, and politicians from Europe and westernized Nations in a forum that would allow for candid and frank discussions of international issues without the fear of being quoted and recorded'. For this reason, the Bilderberg meetings are by invitation only and for the last sixty-six years have been by invitation only and held behind closed doors, either on Rockefeller property or at lavish hotels at various cities across the world.

To ensure its guests are of the desirable sort, i.e. Socialist-leaning/Globalists, the 'Bilderbergers chosen' are first interviewed thoroughly and then recommended by the BB's 'Steering Committee members'. If the requirements are met, they are then officially invited, by the Chairman, to the Bilderberg meeting.

One of the Bilderbergers honorary lifetime chairman's is David Rockefeller, who is also, not coincidentally, the founder of The Trilateral Commission and, by way of the 'Rockefeller family', the CFR (Council on Foreign Relations). We will discuss this Federal Reserve, Trilateral Commission, CFR and Deep State interlock in the coming pages in greater detail. However, the Bilderberg members (not necessarily its guests) have traditionally and exclusively maintained a vested interest in the Rockefeller family's ownership of 'Standard Oil', the Corporation who funded Nazi Germany. As a point of interest, the competition to The Rockefellers 'Standard Oil' is 'Bernhard's Royal Dutch Petroleum', which so happens to be owned by the Rothchild's, it's theoretical and in many cases its real business and Federal Reserve rival on the right-wing faction of the World Court. Now the rivalry between these two families begins to make sense at least in its relationship to its competition over the world's Oil. The Bilderberg Group is heavily involved in manipulation of oil and gas prices, and although they claim not to be publicly, it is one of their primary points of interest with regard to their Globalized economic structure.

During Retinger's funeral in 1960, Sir Edward Bedington-Behrens said:

"I remember Retinger in the United States picking up the telephone and immediately making an appointment with the President, and in Europe he had complete entrée in every political circle as a kind of right acquired through trust, devotion and loyalty he inspired.

"This present window of opportunity, during which a truly peaceful and interdependent world order might be built, will not be open for too long... We are on the verge of a global transformation. All we need is the right major crisis, and the nations will accept the New World Order."

- David Rockefeller, 1994

In 1974, Prince Bernhard of the Netherlands resigned, making Dr. Joseph H. Retinger, the Bilderberg group its first Secretary. Dr. Retinger was the one of the key figures in the formation of the Bilderberg Group in 1954. He was also known as 'His Grey Eminence', and Retinger's full name is Joseph *'Heironymus'* Retinger. The translation of Herionymus from Latin (The Vatican) to English literally means 'Member of the Occult

If the father of the Bilderberg Group having a middle name 'Heironymus' meaning 'member of the occult' seems like a coincidence, it is not. Herionymus was a Jesuit-Roman-Catholic, and his sales pitch for a Bilderberg Group, whose aim was to have a ruling class of elites, with ties to what was then seen as a hostile foreign Communists sympathizer, especially just after fighting Nazi Germany in the early fifties, was met with rebuff and thwarted. Joseph Heironymus Retinger was also seen as a 'Vatican Agent', and accused by many as being an active agent between the Pope, the Father-General, and the Bilderberg Group.

On May 5, 1949, John Heironymus Retinger's crowning achievement amongst internationalists was his ability to unite the European Movement towards the formation of the Council of Europe (It has also been said that the Bilderberg Group has since been responsible for the formation of the European Union and the Euro as the beginnings of a one-world-currency and Government). The Council of Europe's headquarters was strategically well-positioned by the Council Executive Committee, giving Retinger control of the epicenter or western European elites in Strasbourg, Germany.

Being centrally based in Strasbourg, Retinger became deeply involved with the Vatican and its message, being updated and guided by the Jesuit Order. Heironymus as then persuaded by the Vatican to sell the plan for a 'Bilderberg Group' to Premier Georges Clemenceau. The sales pitch was the same then as it is today, to hold secret meetings amongst the most elite and prominent business executives and politicians of what was then considered Eastern Europe (now largely considered to be Western Europe) with the 'tripartite monarchy', or Great Britain, France and Rome (the Western World). All of this was to be achieved under the direction of the Vatican via the Jesuit order. Premier Georges Clemenceau was not impressed, especially with the interconnection between the Vatican and SS Nazi Germany during WW2 being still fresh in the minds of Western Europeans. The Premier saw Retinger's proposal as an active conspiracy with the Jesuit Order and Vatican, and unconditionally rejected Retinger's plan for a 'Bilderberg Group', labeling Joseph Heironymus Retinger a hostile foreign agent of the Vatican.

The Rockefellers messaging is done through its CFR's mind control apparatus. By using propaganda in Main Stream Media and its various 'movements' that change over time, every side of modern topical interest is covered. Interestingly, its agenda is also hidden in plain sight in its very name. It is not a council on foreign relations, it is a council on domestic relations, which effectively control every aspect of American Culture and the various tribalized groups that it has mapped out, in an effort to mind control all tribal groups and very efficiently sway public opinion on the right and left of the American political system. The Rockefeller owned Council on Foreign Relations were originally from New York City. It now has since broadened its horizons to include Washington, DC, and then the entirety of America.

The members of the Bilderberg Group, however are for the most part from various areas of the major Western European

Countries, Greece, Italy, Turkey, Canada and the United States.

The Rockefeller family also owns and operates the Trilateral Commission, which will be explained in the following pages. Its members are also Western European and American/Atlantean/North American, but have expanded its sphere of influence into Asia, particularly Japan and China. Since the Rockefeller operation is essentially a large conglomerate of Banks being guided by the Deep State's 'hidden hand', it would be negligent on their on their part to exclude China and Japan from the New World Order.

Japan especially, being the most maintaining the most dominant currency and Centralized Banks in the world.

Of all the Rockefeller owned Deep State Groups working synergistically, the Bilderberg group is by far the most secretive. they typically drive black limousines or SUV's with tinted windows, front and back. Wherever the Bilderberg meetings are held across the globe, security is virtually impenetrable, and in order to maintain secrecy the Bilderbergers first remove any possible bugging devices, hidden cameras, etcetera. Next, they absolutely clear out the meeting-place, usually a luxury hotel, temporarily remove all its guests, then the employees of the hotel or building. They then allow only their own maids, cooks, waiters, and security into the building. No outsiders are permitted onto the property whatsoever over the course of their meetings, and it has been rumored that in recent years their various armed staff of security officers; The Security used at these meeting includes the CIA, MOSSAD, the Israeli Secret Service and the Defense intel European Union security are told to "shoot to kill", any intruder attempting to break in or trespass on the premises.

There are no written records taken of their discussions, and the protocol for the secrecy of the Bilderberg meetings are, as some of its guests have affirmed that there are no proposed resolutions, no voting takes place and no policy statements are made.

It is also rumored that the Bilderberg's staff has a strict code of conduct in which its 'personal staff' cannot look the Bilderbergers or its guests in the eye, cannot speak to them unless spoken to first, may not address any of those present, and the staff who are right handed must approach the Bilderbergers and its guests from the right, those who are left handed from the left. Nothing is permitted to leak from the meetings from their personal staff or security detail. Leakers are rumored to be threatened, that if any information is leaked from the Bilderberg meetings, they will never find a job in that field for life.

Just to name a few recent high-profile Prime ministers, Presidents and Presidential candidates who have attended the Bilderberg meetings are Trilateralists, George Bush Sr. in 1985, Bill Clinton in 1991, John Kerry, Tony Blair, and Hillary Clinton and Barrack Hussein Obama in 2008 at the Westfield's Marriott Hotel meeting in Chantilly, Virginia Bilderberg meeting.

Although Members of the Bilderberg and their 'sister' organizations, the CFR and the Trilateral Commission (A.K.A. "Child of Bilderberg") are technically in violation of the Logan Act, for discussing foreign policy with hostile foreign entities, and The Constitution of various monarchies throughout Europe restricts members of their royal families from engaging in any discussion of policy or anything of political influence in their countries; unfortunately, it seems these laws have been effectively bypassed and worked around due to the fact that the CFR, Trilateral Commission, and the Bilderberg Group is a CIA operation, completely immune to Nation Laws. These groups are effectively only subject to International law.

Although it has also been alleged that these three groups are a drug dealer's consortium of international bankers who control the private central banks of the world, gun running, oil markets, terrorism, plots for globalized depopulation, and economic instability in Markets; it is important to remember that these groups, especially the Bilderberg Group, does not actively discuss any of their more sinister operations with their guests, who are not privy to much of the reasons behind their agenda. Instead, the guests of these meetings are most likely only told a story of the philanthropic and beneficial nature of their agenda for the purpose of maintaining secrecy and the overall effectiveness of indirectly achieving their end game.

"The drive of the Rockefellers and their allies is to create a one-world government combining supercapitalism and Communism under the same tent, all under their control.... Do I mean conspiracy? Yes, I do. I am convinced there is such a plot, international in scope, generations old in planning, and incredibly evil in intent."

- Congressman Larry P. McDonald, 1975

"We are grateful to The Washington Post, The New York Times, Time Magazine and other great publications whose directors have attended our meetings and respected their promises

of discretion for almost forty years. It would have been impossible for us to develop our plan for the world if we had been subject to the bright lights of publicity during those years. But, the work is now much more sophisticated and prepared to march towards a world government. The supranational sovereignty of an intellectual elite and world bankers is surely preferable to the national autodetermination practiced in past centuries."

- David Rockefeller, 1991

"This unprecedented period of European cooperation is more than a product of simple nation-state diplomacy. One of the key institutions that has fostered unity and cooperation with the Atlantic Community beyond the old concepts has been the Bilderberg Group. I tell you frankly that I am deeply alarmed today over the possibility that a right-wing reaction may draw some sections of capital so far away from our traditions as to imperil the entire structure of American life as we know it."

- Pasymowski

THE TRILATERAL COMMISSON

"The Trilateral Commission is international and is intended to be the vehicle for multinational consolidation of the commercial and banking interests by seizing control of the political government of the United States. The Trilateral Commission represents a skillful, coordinated effort to seize control and consolidate the four centers of power - political, monetary, intellectual, and ecclesiastical."

- Barry Goldwater, 1979

The Trilateral Commission was established in 1973 with the help of David Rockefeller and Zbigniew Brzezinski. The Rockefeller's already had a hand in the foundation of the Bilderberg Group and the Council on Foreign Relations.

David Rockefeller was at that time, Chairman of Chase Manhattan Bank, Global financier, and one of the twelve principal owners of the twelve Federal Reserve Banks of the United States of America. Zbigniew Brzezinski was the so-called intellectual of the operation, writing the book entitled, 'Between Two Ages: America's Role in the Technetronic Era', that outlined the Columbia University Professor's, Zbigniew Brzezinski's vision of a Globalized economic world, which very quickly caught the attention of David Rockefeller; spurring what is now the Globalized patriarchal system of the 'Deep State' and a more far-reaching and interwoven definition of the 'New World Order.'

The Trilateral Commission Magazine Trialogue states that: 'The Trilateral Commission was formed in 1973 by private citizens of Western Europe, Japan and North America to foster closer cooperation among these three regions on common problems. It seeks to improve public understanding of such problems, to support proposals for handling them jointly, and to nurture habits and practices of working together among these regions.'

Brzezinski, a professor at Columbia University, a seer of sorts on the perfection of a one-world economic structure; wrote numerous books on his globalized vision of the future and in particular, Between Two Ages became the de facto 'Bible on Globalization' and its international economic and political policy structure for the Trilateral Commission. Brzezinski was thereafter appointed the first executive director of the Trilateral Commission upon its foundation in 1973. Just three years after the Commission was formed, Brzezinski was then appointed by President Jimmy Carter in 1976 as Assistant to the President for National Security Affairs.

In line with the Bilderberg Group and CFR, these Trilateralists members are also similarly comprised of a select few of the world's elite prominent politicians, professors, main stream media, and business moguls, the heads of prominent labor unions and international bankers. These members however are not by invitation, but are widely believed to be the Bilderberg Groups permanent ranking club members who hold the annual Bilderberger meetings and policy makers for the second tier of elite guests of the BB's meetings.

The Trilateral Commissions ranking club members are comprised of around 300 members who are proportionately divided into three groups of one hundred men from each group. One hundred from Europe, 100 from Japan and another 100 from North America.

Brzezinski alliance between Western Europe, North America, and The Japanese/Eurasian markets is the Deep State's left-wing faction of politics, being essentially founded upon older Marxist and Alinsky model's for Global Economic reform: "Resist as it might, the American system is compelled gradually to accommodate itself to this emerging international context, with the U.S. government called upon to negotiate, to guarantee, and, to some extent, to protect the various arrangements that have been contrived even by private business."

Brzezinski writings described mankind's movement into four stages of evolution:

I. The first stage was described as 'Religious' (No-

Government)

"universalism provided by the acceptance of the idea that man's destiny is essentially in God's hands" with an earthly "narrowness derived from massive ignorance, illiteracy, and a vision confined to the immediate environment."

I. The second stage described as 'Nationalism' (Nation-State-Capitalism) Christian equality before the law *"marked another giant step in the progressive redefinition of man's nature and place in our world."*

I. The third stage described as 'Marxism' (Nation-State-Communism)

"represents a further vital and creative stage in the maturing of man's universal vision."

I. The final stage described as 'The Technetronic Era - result of American-Communist evolutionary transformations' (Globalized-Communist-One-World-Government)

Brzezinski believed the U.S. Government's Nation-State was outmoded and could be undermined over time by multinational Corporations: "Tension is unavoidable as man strives to assimilate the new into the framework of the old. For a time, the established framework resiliently integrates the new by adapting it in a more familiar shape. But at some point, the old framework becomes overloaded. The newer input can no longer be redefined into traditional forms, and eventually it asserts itself with compelling force. Today, though, the old framework of international politics - with their spheres of influence, military alliances between nation-states, the fiction of sovereignty, doctrinal conflicts arising from nineteenth century crises - is clearly no longer compatible with reality. The approaching two-hundredth anniversary of the Declaration of Independence could justify the call for a national constitutional convention to reexamine the nation's formal institutional framework. Either 1976 or 1989 - the two-hundredth an anniversary of the Constitution - could serve as a suitable target date culminating a national dialogue on the relevance of existing arrangements. Realism, however, forces us to recognize that the necessary political innovation will not come from direct constitutional reform, desirable as that would be. The needed change is more likely to develop incrementally and less overtly...in keeping with the American tradition of blurring distinctions between public and private institution. The "nation-state as a fundamental unit of man's organized life has ceased to be the principal creative force: International banks and multinational corporations are acting and planning in terms that are far in advance of the political concepts of the nation-state."

David Rockefeller's idea for the formation of a Trilateral Commission was presented to the already formed Bilderberg Group in 1972 in Knokke, Belgium, although the planning for the Commission was already underway and deliberated upon privately at meetings held in New York City, at the Rockefeller's Pocantico Hills estate. On the surface, the idea of a unification of the East and West seemed innocuous and harmless, as it was meant to, but upon further inspection, Senator Barry Goldwater, one of the Trilateralists foremost critics described the Commission quite differently: "The Trilateral organization created by David Rockefeller was a surrogate, the members selected by Rockefeller, its purposes defined by Rockefeller, its funding supplied by David Rockefeller screened and selected every individual who was invited participate. The Commission's purpose is to engineer an enduring partnership among the ruling classes of North America, Western Europe and Japan —hence the term 'Trilateral', in order to safeguard the interests of Western capitalism in an explosive world. The private commission is attempting to mold public policy and construct a framework for international stability in the coming decades. To put it simply, Trilateralists are saying: The people, governments and economies of all nations must serve the needs of multinational banks and corporations. In short, Trilateralism is the current attempt by ruling elites to manage both dependence and democracy - at home and abroad."

After the formalities were in place with the Bilderberger's, Brzezinski and Rockefeller just needed to choose the brokers of the New World Order who they saw fit to govern The Trilateral Commission. These Shadow Government's New World Elite would shape our country, world, and its policies for the next forty years! The New World Order officially began with President Jimmy Carter when he took office in 1977, and was temporarily interrupted, as the Trilateralists saw it, by Ronald Reagan. Although, according to David Rockefeller's account in his book Memoirs written in 2002even Reagan was under their control and guidance after four years in office: "President Reagan ultimately came to understand Trilaterals value and invited the entire membership to a reception at the White House in April 1984"

From Carter to Obama, notwithstanding the four-year interim of President Ronald Reagan's first term in office, there have been not four, but six Deep State - New World Order U.S.

Presidents severing in office under the steering hidden hand of the Trilateral Commission.

In 1973, Brzezinski's vision for a Trilateralist President seemed to have Jimmy Carter in mind three years ahead of the Presidential primaries: "The Democratic candidate in 1976 will have to emphasize work, the family, religion and, increasingly, patriotism... The new conservatism will clearly not go back to laissez faire. It will be a philosophical conservatism. It will be a kind of conservative statism or managerism. There will be conservative values but a reliance on a great deal of co-determination between state and the corporations."

The Trilateral Commission's primary objective as a newly formed Governance, foreign to the 'nation-state', was to groom the right Trilateralist and insert him into the Oval Office. Rockefeller and Brzezinski set out to select the next President of the United States, and managed to narrow their list down to a dozen or so candidates. Although the list mostly consisted of Democrats, there were also left-leaning Republican 'Internationalists' who were considered. Rockefeller decided that the best way to groom its chosen U.S. President, was to have him first become a member of the Commission, a 'Trilateralist'; A man who was willing to fully cooperate with their New World Order agenda. It didn't take long to find their perfect Presidential Candidate, The Democrat Governor of Georgia, Jimmy Carter.

Carter was not able to attend a meeting in person, as far as what is known to the public, however letters relating to the correspondence of the meeting were reprinted in the Trilateral Commission's official Magazine, '*Trialogue*':

"It gives me special pleasure to send greetings to all of you gathering for the Trilateral Commission meeting in Tokyo. I have warm memories of our meeting in Tokyo some eighteen months ago, and am sorry I cannot be with you now. My active service on the Commission since its inception in 1973 has been a splendid experience for me, and it provided me with excellent opportunities to come to know leaders in our three regions. As I emphasized in my campaign, a strong partnership among us is of the greatest importance. We share economic, political and security concerns that make it logical we should seek ever-increasing cooperation and understanding. And this cooperation is essential not only for our three regions, but in 'the global search for a more just and equitable world order.' I hope to see you on the occasion of your next meeting in Washington, and I look forward to receiving reports on your work in Tokyo. - Jimmy Carter"

Carter's response to the Trilateral Commission seems to mirror what can only be explained as, Trilateralist code which is also found in Brzezinski's letter:

"The Trilateral Commission has meant a great deal to me over the last few years. It has been the stimulus for intellectual creativity and a source of personal satisfaction. I have formed close ties with new friends and colleagues in all three regions, ties which I value highly and which I am sure will continue. I remain convinced that, on the larger architectural issues of today, collaboration among our regions is of the utmost necessity. This collaboration must be dedicated to the fashioning of a more just and equitable world order. This will require a prolonged process, but I think we can look forward with confidence and take some pride in the contribution which the Commission is making. Zbigniew Brzezinski."

Carter apparently spoke the magic words in his letter to the Trilateral Commission, using the phrase, 'a more just and equitable world order,' which is also found verbatim in Brzezinski's letter. Jimmy Carter now had passed the test, and would go on to be the next unelected U.S. President.

'Brazilian newspaper Vega', September 1974:

"How would you define this New World Order?"

Brzezinski answered: "When I speak of the present international system I am referring to relations in specific fields, most of all among the Atlantic countries; commercial, military, mutual security relations, involving the international monetary fund, NATO etc. We need to change the international system for a global system in which new, active and creative forces recently developed - should be integrated. This system needs to include Japan, Brazil, the oil producing countries, and even the USSR, to the extent which the Soviet Union is willing to participate in a global system."

In the 1970's David Rockefeller was known to have a personal portfolio in Atlanta real estate and connections to the city's elite, and coincidently, five years before the Presidential Campaign of 76' began, Rockefeller befriended Jimmy Carter in 1971 inviting him to his Chase Manhattan Bank for dinner.

While James Carter seemed to be at the top of the list for their 77' Unelected President, Florida Govender at that time, Reuben Askew was also another trilateral who was competing for the Presidential job interview as well. Brzezinski recounts just how close this Presidential job interview between was: "It was a close thing between Carter and Askew, but we were impressed that Carter had opened up trade offices for the state of Georgia in Brussels and Tokyo. That seemed to fit perfectly into the concept of the Trilateral."

But by 1975 it looked as though Rockefeller had made up his mind when Brzezinski gave Carter his endorsement before the Trilateral Commission in Kyoto, Japan. Senator Barry Goldwater recalls: "Rockefeller and Brzezinski found Carter to be their ideal candidate. They helped him win the Democratic nomination and the presidency. To accomplish this purpose, they mobilized the money-power of the Wall Street bankers, the intellectual influence of the academic community—which is subservient to the wealth of the great tax-free foundations—and the media controllers represented in the membership of the CFR and the Trilateralists."

"The real menace of our Republic is the invisible government which like a giant octopus sprawls its slimy legs over our cities states and nation. At the head is a small group of banking houses generally referred to as 'international bankers.' This little coterie run our government for their own selfish ends. It operates under cover of a self-created screen and seizes our executive officers, legislative bodies, schools, courts, newspapers and every agency created for the public protection."

- John F. Hylan

When Carter became President in 1977, it should come as no surprise that those that made him President were rewarded by appointments to his Cabinet and Senior Staff. Brzezinski became President Carter's head of the National Security Council. Walter Mondale, who was also an obscure figure before 1975, but was also a fellow Trilateralist, became Vice

President; and it is estimated that nineteen members of the one-hundred that represented the United States Trilateral Commission became prominent political figures during the Carter Administration.

"For you see, the world is governed by very different personages from what is imagined by those who are not behind the scenes."

- Benjamin Disraeli

The image given to Jimmy Carter by the Rockefeller CFR-run media as a Presidential Nominee was very similar to that of Barrack Hussein Obama in that he was not only a virtually unknown political figure before running for President, he was also given the illusion (by the CFR-run media) of being a political outsider, innocent to the corrupt world of politics; when in fact the opposite was true. The Parallels shared between these two Presidents are strikingly similar and although President Obama is not a known Trilateralist per-se, he did also meet with the Trilateral Commission via the Bilderberg group in 2007. Many believe he was also injected into office; the very same way Jimmy Carter was in 1977.

Time Magazine named Obama 'Person of the Year' in 2008 and in 1977 Jimmy Carter was also named 'Man of the Year' for no other reason than being elected President of the United States. Hedley Donovan (also a Trilateralist) was editor-in-chief of the magazine in 1977, but instead of citing Carter's membership to the Commission, provides a false impression of President Carter being an outsider, naïve to politics: "As he searched for Cabinet appointees, Carter seemed at times hesitant and frustrated disconcertingly out of character. His lack of ties to Washington and the Party Establishment - qualities that helped raise him to the White House - carry potential dangers. He does not know the Federal Government or the pressures it creates. He does not really know the politicians whom he will need to help him run the country."

The New York Times, however characterized Carter's ascendance to the Presidency as:

"(Brzezinski) was the first guy in the Community to pay attention to Carter, to take him seriously. He spent time with Carter, talked to him, sent him books and articles, educated him." "While the Community as a whole was looking elsewhere, to Senators Kennedy and Mondale... it paid off. Brzezinski, with Gardner, is now the leading man on Carter's foreign policy task force."

"The interests behind the Bush Administration, such as the CFR, The Trilateral Commission - founded by Brzezinski for David Rockefeller - and the Bilderberger Group, have prepared for and are now moving to implement open world dictatorship within the next five years. They are not fighting against terrorists. They are fighting against citizens."

- Dr. Johannes B. Koeppl, PhD

Freemasons & Druids

"Throughout Gaul there are two classes of persons of definite account and dignity. As for the common folk, they are treated almost as slaves, venturing naught of themselves, never taken into counsel. The more part of them, oppressed as they are either by debt, or by the heavy weight of tribute, or by the wrongdoing of the more powerful men, commit themselves in slavery to the nobles, who have, in fact, the same rights over them as masters over slaves. <u>Of the two classes above mentioned one consists of Druids, the other of knights. The former are concerned with divine worship, the due performance of (p337) sacrifices, public and private, and the interpretation of ritual questions</u>: a great number of young men gather about them for the sake of instruction and hold them in great honor. In fact, it is they who decide in almost all disputes, public and private; and if any crime has been committed, or murder done, or there is any disposes about succession or boundaries, they also decide it, determining rewards and penalties: if any person or people does not abide by their decision, they ban such from sacrifice, which is their heaviest penalty. Those that are so banned are reckoned as impious and criminal; all men move out of their path and shun their approach and conversation, for fear they may get some harm from their contact, and no justice is done if they seek it, no distinction falls to their share. Of all these Druids one is chief, who has the highest authority among them."

- Julius Caesar, Gallic War, Book VI

HISTORY OF FREEMASONRY

Before delving into the minutia of the hidden history of Freemasonry and its roots, which a great many people genuinely believe to be Christ-like, while another group of equally as many critics unquestionably understand it only to be a Satanic cult veiled under the guise of 'Illumination'; let's begin with Julius Caesar's written portrayal of the Druids and the ancient civilization of Gaul (Celtic England) which can be traced back to the 3rd century B.C.; letting the reader decide for himself what is at the core of Masonry. It is also worth noting that there is a very real connection with the teachings of the Druid people of Gaul and modern-day Freemasonry.

The Druid's came nearly two-thousand years before the Freemasons had any known records or documentation in 1646 (later established officially in 1717) and although little is known of them, the parallels between these two groups are not only strikingly similar, but undeniably connected.

One of the first similarities which can be linked to both the Druids and Freemasons is most notably found in their shared philosophical belief in the power of secrecy. While the Masons are inherently secretive, their rationale for this secrecy is claimed to be due to their fear of oppression from the Church of England (Separation of Church and State). The Druids, however came before Christ – and had no reason for secrecy outside of a shared vision of a society where all knowledge was only meant for the elite ruling class and its patriarchal system.

The Druidic system of governance had two opposing and warring factions who were also very similarly unified in politics and in its elitism amongst its patriarchy; The Knights and the

Druids, as Julius Caesar described. While the Druids seemed to have slightly more power over the Knights of the Gaul's Kingdom, the Knights served as an acting balance of power, so to speak, creating a right and left duality in Government. This is also nearly identical to the Freemasonic system which also has two equal, yet opposing 'rites,' the York and the Scottish Rite. The York Rite does not require a belief in 'Christ,' while the Scottish Rite does.

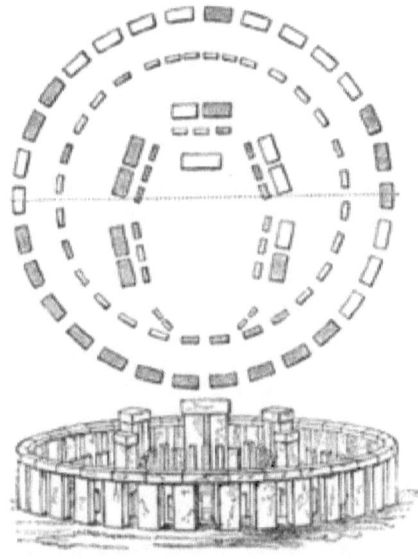

The third and fourth undeniably similar tradition between Druid and Freemasonic systems are in their mastery of the craft of stone masonry, their building of elaborate structures, built with occult-like symbolism and or symmetrical polygonal patterns. The forth similarity can be found in their advancements in mathematics, and as it pertains to exactly how they see mathematical patterns as holding some supernatural or paranormal force, which it holds in its ritualistic pagan energy in these magmatically choreographed formations. For example, on the left we have Stonehenge, built just outside of Wiltshire, England and above we have the Pentagon, which can be found just outside of Washington, D.C. Both structures are encoded with the number 33, with Stonehenge being exactly 33 meters across. Both also echo similarities in design, with relationships in their astrological alignments, chambers, turning quarters, and possible sacrificial stones. Although the Pentagon is 25 times the size of Stonehenge, it is also clearly built to scale. Another fascinating similarity is between the construction of the Pentagon, Stonehenge and the Great Pyramids of Giza (also similar to the Pyramids built worldwide). All three structures have corresponding measurements from the top to the king's chamber at its centermost point, six degrees off center from its respective due north. The Pyramids, Stonehenge, and the Pentagon are also three megalithic degrees from the center of Washington D.C., with respective measurements of 377 and 366 feet.

Franklin Delano Roosevelt was an architect, a 33rd degree Freemason and first Presidential American-Socialist, and insisted that the Pentagon was to be built immediately upon his request, just two years after World War II had begun, and was to be explicitly built at a point called 'Hells Bottom' in Washington D.C., positioned at the perfect angle and dimensions as it relates to Stonehenge. Moreover, as some may already know, September 11th has long been a Freemasonic holy day, so it will come as no surprise that FDR had the Pentagon under construction on September 11th, 1941. Roosevelt did all of this against the advice of the United States Military for the express purpose of building 'The New

Jerusalem' giving the Druids and Freemason's 3000 years from the time of Solomon to find a city that is worthy to rule over the world as the Capital city of the New World Order's one-world-government, our nation's capital, Washington D.C. The Pentagon was built twenty-five times larger than Stonehenge, to scale, and with the ancient measurement of a 'megalith,' arching '33' megalithic degrees between the three centers of (the Pentagon) the Jefferson Memorial, and the Capital building.

Stonehenge is believed to be 6000 years old, and among some of the more unorthodox possible theories as to how it was built are that the magician Merlin levitated the megalithic stones into place or that they were set into place by giants (Ananke or Nephilim). Although there is reason to believe that these stones may be magnetically charged with some sort of acoustic energy, it is more likely that the megalithic stones that make up Stonehenge may have been floated into place across the Irish Sea. In any case, what's more, important is that it is believed that Stonehenge was the epicenter for the Druidic rituals practiced during the ancient Pagan holiday known as 'Vulcania' on August 23rd, during the ceremonial 'Summer of Human Sacrifice and Consumption.'

How does human sacrifice tie into Druidic history, Stonehenge, the Pentagon, and Freemasonry? Stonehenge, The Freemasonic Statue of Liberty, George Washington's National Masonic Memorial (separated by 333 miles), Yale University, Harvard University, Wall Street, 9/11- ground zero, Washington D.C., Philadelphia, New York City, Boston, Baltimore, Helliwell Provincial Hornby Island in British Columbia, The Forbidden city of China, Sandy Hook, the

CIA, The White House, DOD, the Library of Congress, the Supreme Court, and you guessed it, the Pentagon all line up with the '33rd Parallel of death', which is a ley-line or 'global line' that begins from the North, at Stonehenge, and extends southward along the U.S. eastern seaboard to its southernmost

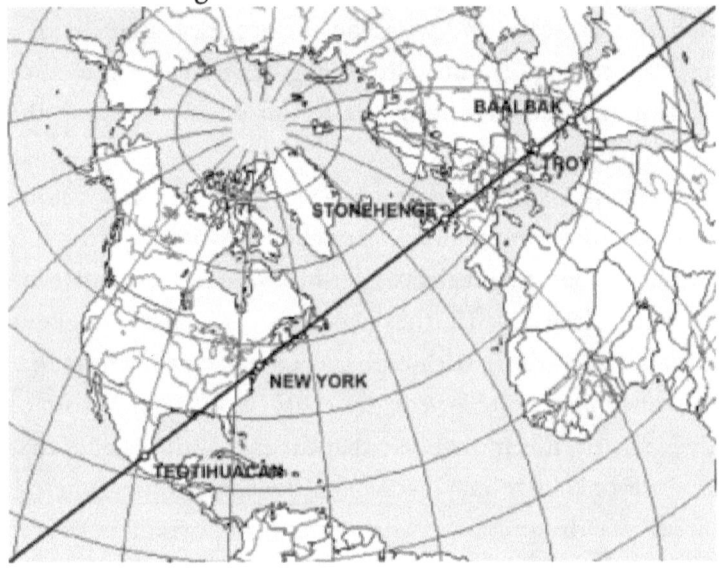

point at Teotihuacan, Mexico, 5,458 miles away. The 'Sirius Ley-Line' (not pictured here) intersects with this 33rd Parallel ley-line extending through Houston, Texas (JFK assassination) as it passes through Memphis, Tennessee (MLK assassination), into Japan. This 'Sirius ley-line' is also known as the 'Arcadia Meridian' and it is also believed to have intersecting points that form a man-made, Freemasonic grid or triangle of Sacrifice that does not coincidentally begin and end at Stonehenge and Teotihuacan, Mexico's Temple of Quetzalcoatl at the Pyramid of the Sun and Moon or 'The Avenue of Death'. The Romans celebrated it at Stonehenge after conquering the Gaul's who began the tradition before them, beginning the celebration on May 1st through the 15th, Witches Day, A.K.A. the festivity of the Shrine to 'Vulcan.' Of course, these human sacrificial rituals have always been celebrated, most notably at the sacrificial stone of these Megalithic stone structures—made by Freemasonic-Druids and pre-Aztec pagans at the Teotihuacan's Temple of Quetzalcoatl!

Is the 33rd Meridian a sacrificial line honoring a six-thousand-year-old tradition of human sacrifice with Pagan and Satanic roots that span nearly six-thousand miles from Stonehenge to the Pyramid of the Sun? Were the Druids and the pre-Aztecan civilization, who have both long since died out, working together in an ancient Globalized world similar to today's? If so was this by design or merely a coincidence? An understanding of recent history does, in fact, hold the answer. Freemasons do indeed wish to bring back the one whom they call the 'Grand Architect of the Universe'; to summon 'God' back to earth to recreate what they herald to be 'the age of wisdom' to fuse the scientific and the metaphysical, ideally under a one-world Government.

The Secret History of the 'Brotherhood of the Diamond'

As has been clearly stated, the architects of Masonry and its roots were established long before any of its earliest known records were discovered or upon its formal inception in 1623 The Freemason globalized philosophy has reshaped the function of science, mathematics, the educational system worldwide, all governments, its leaders, politicians, elites, secret societies, nearly every religious institution (international and local), and even the geographical landscape and positioning of many of the major cities throughout the world. Masons are not only the architects of buildings, but they have also been the architects of our world, lurking behind everything imaginable which now encompasses it.

The hero of the Freemasons is a metaphorical character named Hiram Abiff who is at the heart of all Masonic teachings and is believed by those who practice its rites to be the architect of King Solomon's Temple. Although Biblical scholars denounce this belief as heresy, since no actual reference to this man is mentioned in the Torah or Bible, a great many Masons believe Hiram Abiff was a literal person and not figurative at all. Critics of this belief argue that Hiram is the Masons very own Jesus Christ, created merely to suit the needs of their Secret Society.

As the legend goes, Hyrum Abiff is the Widow's son, the master builder of King Solomon's temple. The Widow is believed by some to signify Mary, the mother of Jesus. Since Mary was married to Joseph, there would be no conceivable reason for Mary to be a widow unless Masons hold the belief that Mary is the wife of a dead father (Since Jesus is considered to be 'The Son of God' by Judeo-Christians, this Freemasonic analogy could only mean the son of a dead God). According to the legend of King Solomon was given the design and dimensions of his temple directly from God and Hyrum Abiff, its master builder, was the only other man who knew of its secret design, power, and secrets which it held. Abiff (Masonic-Jesus) is then threatened by three men ('the three wise men,' Ignorance, fanaticism and Tyranny) who demanded the secret knowledge behind King Solomon's Temple. The Three Mason builders of the Temple believe there was a code word that carries God's divine plan and that if they are able to receive the code will also receive Divine or magical God-like powers. The Three Stone cutters ask Hyrum for the secret word for months and are not answered, so finally, as Abiff approaches the east door of the Temple to pray; one of the three men accost him demanding the Secret. According to the legend, Hyrum Abiff tells him that they will be given it when they have accomplished their work, and the Temple is complete. Hyrum's throat is then cut with the Masons stone, when the second builder demands 'the word,' again Abiff refuses to give the secret and is then struck with the Mason's Square. The Third Mason asks yet again and is refused, this time Abiff is killed with another Square. As he is dying, he yells, 'who will help the widow's son?'

The rituals, indoctrination, and initiation in the Freemasonry, or the 'Brotherhood of the Diamond' (Incidentally, the mystery of the Diamond is perhaps the most hidden of all Freemasonic secrets, but is important to understand, since the Pyramids are associated with Freemasons - their ever-present Pyramidal symbols and Washington D.C.'s boundaries do not form a square, but a Diamond!) all center around the theme of Hiram Abiff legend. The purpose given by Freemasons for the importance of this metaphorical teaching put into practice with Masonic garb and regalia, fake beards, and costumes, etc. is one, to stress importance of 'Death before Dishonor '; and secondly, to imitate the rebirth of its initiates being reborn, as Jesus Christ, but instead by Hiram Abiff, welcoming their members into a pre-Illuminati World Order

THESIS

The origins of Stone Masonry began with the first King of England, King Athelstan in the 10th century A.D. These

Stone Masons were not merely stonecutters who decided to claim freedom from the Church, quite the opposite, they were very much the Church itself; bound with a very real interlock with the Roman Catholic Church, as they are today with the Jesuit-Catholic Church of the Vatican. They were the founding fathers, so to speak, of modern Masonry today, hence the derivation of their name Freemasons. The idea of fusing Democratic-Socialism, Metaphysical Mysticism with the hard science of Geometry, and Kabalistic mathematics has now become the cornerstone if you will of modern-day Freemasonry. By the late 1700's the conditions were ripe for an Adam Weishaupt to overhaul and radicalize the already extreme world of the Freemasons, bringing the Masons deeper into the full-blown practice of Satanism, no longer being shrouded in mystical teachings and what the Masons like to call 'their journey.' As explained in Volume I of the History of the Deep State, the Order of the Illuminati made no 'bones' about what they believed was indeed at the heart of Masonry, with the new order of Weishaupt being established and accepted at every Freemasonic Temple and lodge around the world by 1776 and extending into the second Order of Death, with the advent of Skull and Bones in 1832, then at last being perfected and ushered into the New World Order in 1991; when the Secret of the brotherhood of the Diamond was finally put to rest, being fully exposed in plain sight!

Washington's CIA

"Yale has influenced the Central Intelligence Agency more than any other University, giving the CIA the atmosphere of a class reunion. Bondsmen have been foremost among the "spooks" building the CIA's "haunted house."

- Gaddis Smith, professor at Yale

Recently, there has been a lot of speculation and debate about the CIA being where the Deep State begins and ends, working together with the FBI and other intelligence agencies in the United States and intel around the world. There are two reasons why this is not true, one we've had centralized intelligence since the days of George Washington and two, Centralized Intelligence has always been just another addition to the vast web of Deep State components that work cohesively against the best interests of America and Americans; who have been defined by law as 'Enemies of The State'.

Furthermore, the CIA was not technically established under President Harry Truman in 1947. It was already in place but known as the OSS, or the Office of Strategic Services in 1945, which was also formed for the proposed reason for having a need for enhancing foreign intelligence gathering during World War II. Both the OSS and the CIA were an attempt at replicating an 'American version' of the British Secret Service (MI6).

Furthermore, before becoming President (even before the declaration of Independence or the beginning of the Revolutionary War!), George Washington established the first Centralized Intelligence Agency with the assistance of Nathan Hale, who later went on to become 'Chief of Intelligence' under President George Washington, the 'Father of American Intelligence', A.K.A. 'The Fox', A.K.A. '711'.

Washington's first central intelligence agency was established with help from three graduates of Yale University, forming the "Culper Spy Ring." George Washington was not an incredible General by any means, in fact, he was a horrible General, often falsely credited with winning the Revolutionary War, which was in fact, entirely fueled and funded by the Order of the Illuminati of Bavaria. The legend/fable states that Washington was able to defeat the British army with only a mere 1,800 ragtag troops with no uniforms, supplies, proper training, and inferior weaponry; all of this was achieved against the greatest military in the world at that time, the British Army. Despite being indoctrinated in schools at a young age, take a minute to consider if this is even possible? Is it possible that it was just an illusion to gain favor with the American public? A Revolutionary war was not popular with the Colonialists. It was not worth fighting for taxes, tariffs, or for any other reason. In fact, it has been estimated that less than one-third of the Colonialists approved of a war at all! The untold truth is Americans simply didn't see the value or need for it. The American Revolution was simply a war for the 'elites' of America, creating a false perception of a 'people's revolution' against a despotic British Monarchy; in reality, it was simply a war against the Christian tradition of the British and its Church and State. Why? Because the founding fathers were anti-Christian and as much as we would love to believe the false narrative of a God-fearing group of men, this Central Intelligence tale is simply not true. The only 'Independence' that was actually formed was by the elites of the Order of

Illuminati from the Roman Catholic Church – forming a 'New World Order' in the 'New World' (also not coincidentally founded as the American Revolution' was on July 4th, 1776 – How convenient to have both the birth of the New World and the founding of the Illuminati on the same day!). The 'American Revolution' was no revolution at all, inasmuch as we understand a revolution to mean 'a people's revolt against an oppressive system of Governance.' The American Revolution was the first Deep State psyops operation perpetrated on the American public. Of course, after the British signed the Paris peace treaty and submitted to the New World, no one even noticed what had actually happened, or questioned why it did!

"The necessity of procuring good intelligence is apparent and need not be further urged – All that remains for me to add is, that you keep the whole matter as secret as possible. For upon Secrecy, Success depends in most Enterprises of the kind, and for want of it, they are generally defeated, however well planned and promising a favorable issue."

- George Washington, First Intelligence Chief of the United States, 1777

In an age where President Trump has rightfully called out a fake Media, where people are beginning to understand that much of the news we are being told on a daily basis is not only false, but worse it is pure propaganda; one should then begin to question, how long has this been taking place, and if all of American History itself was just a series of false flag events, staged crises, and false narratives for the long-term programming of the American public:

"We'll know our disinformation program is complete when everything the American public believes is false."

- William Casey, CIA Director, 1981

Examples of these false narratives beginning as early as the 'American Revolution' and being committed deliberately and falsely against the American people can most notably be found in the writings of Thomas Paine. Unraveling this hoax begins with the rhyming mnemonic quote by John Adams, "Without the pen of Paine, the sword of Washington would have been wielded in vain, then with the commanding statement that: "History is to ascribe the Revolution to Thomas Paine" – suggesting that the false narrative of a 'fight for Independence' would not be complete without first giving the American public the writings of Paine's 'Common Sense' before the lie of Washington fighting in battle for America; which he absolutely did not! In fact, this fairy tale is so incredibly 'fake' that Washington did not only ever engage in any battle of any kind, he most likely never got his hands dirty at all, being far too busy being primed and proper inside a Centralized Intelligence/Secret Society/Freemasonic Temple, discussing ways to deceive and fool the American public.

If this is not enough to convince you of the most revered of founding fathers, Thomas Paine, who is often credited as being the man who made American Independence possible, was nothing but Anti-Christian, consider his writings from 'Age of Reason':

"But when I see throughout the greater part of this book (the Bible) scarcely anything but a history of the grossest vices and a collection of the most paltry and contemptible tales, I cannot dishonor my Creator by calling it by his name....I do not believe in the creed professed by the Jewish Church, by the Roman Church, by the Greek Church, by the Turkish

Church, by the Protestant Church, nor by any church that I know of. My own mind is my own church... <u>It is the fable of Jesus Christ, as told in the New Testament, and the wild and visionary doctrine raised thereon, which I contend.</u>"

Paine was also good friends with founding father, Benjamin Franklin. History also gives a false impression of Franklin as being some sort of Christian hero, when in fact he was not a Christian, nor a hero; he was the unofficial Ambassador to France, making regular visits there meeting with the Illuminati who conspired with Franklin to overthrow the British Crown, abolish the Roman Catholic Church from America, along with all religion in Government (under the guise of the need for separation of 'Church and State'). You see, the founding fathers were not seeking freedom from a despotic and abusive British Government, as Historians have falsely ascribed; instead it was simply a hostile takeover of the Roman-Catholic Church which was spearheaded by the elite 'enlightenment thinkers' of Bavaria, France, and the New World – 'The Founding Fathers'.

The story begins after Benjamin Franklin's plotting with the French Illuminati to overthrow the British Government, not by force, but through a series of traps laid by the French Governments Illuminati, its Naval units and Washington's first Intelligence agency, the Culper Ring. The idea was to give the general public the illusion of war and uprising, when it was nothing more than deceptive tactics to gain control over the British Government, then to make it look like a miraculous event had taken place, which could only be perceived as though God himself was involved. From that point on, generations must always look back at the founding fathers in reverence and view Conventional Christianity as the same occultist Christianity that those great men who founded America did. The effects of this lie forever changed the way the world would perceive a political and Freemasonic and Illuminati based system of 'Christianity.' Here's how the narrative unfolded:

By the summer of 1774 The Order of the Illuminati, after being banished from the Kingdom of Bavaria, Germany for plotting to overthrow the Government, decided to it was time to set their sights on a far easier and expansive target to exploit and conquer. Europe would be easy, being already so completely immersed with Freemasonry throughout the region; but first, it needed to put the strongest power of Western Europe in its place, England and its western counterpart, America or 'The New World.' Then with the help of France, it would use its wealth and Naval Superiority to overthrow England's America, while bankrupting France, then come back to finish it off during the 'French Revolution.' America was the key, being the center of strategic power, and already known as the Citadel of Freedom for the world, America. The Illuminati could take out two birds with one stone, England and America; while liquidating a greedy French Government for helping fund the invasion; making three hostile invasions of the most powerful countries of the world in less than a decade look easy.

While Benjamin Franklin worked out the details for the French backup necessary to win the Revolutionary War, Washington, also known as Agent 711, formed America's first Central Intelligence Agency, the 'Culper Spy Ring.' Washington assembled the spy ring in 1776, shortly after the signing of the Declaration of Independence. With the help of Yale's very own, Nathan Hale. Hale volunteered but was quickly found out and hung by the British army for treason. Major Benjamin Tallmadge would be Hale's replacement for Washington's CIA and given the alias name John Bolton, and the number 721. George Washington would be assigned the number 711. The British were #72 and were headquartered in New York City. NYC was given the code number 727. The operation officially began in 1778 during the British re-occupation, if you will, since there was not a war at all, it would be more accurate to describe the Revolutionary War as an intelligence operation, with Deep State counterintelligence to make it appear to be an incredible and heroic war. The Culper Ring's operation took place mostly on Long Island, code number 728. Essentially all of America's founding fathers were members of the spy ring and complicit in the first American intelligence/psyops operation. However, the network of real spies, informants and disinformants were formed using tightly knit friendships, families, tailors, farmers, tailors, churches, store owners, taverns, merchants, tailors, farmers, secret societies and Freemasonic lodges throughout New York City.

At the heart of the Operation was a group who grew up together, attending the same one-room Episcopal Church-run school in Setauket, New York (#729). Benjamin Tallmadge's (A.K.A. John Bolton, #721) and Nathan Hale of the Yale Alumni (Incidentally, Hale's grandmother was XXX Yale, whom Yale University was named after and Tallmadge and Hale would later become roommates at Yale– not a random coincidence!) were the head agents the operation under the

Fox, George Washington. Tallmadge appointed trusted his best friend, Abraham Woodhull (Samuel Culper Sr. 722).

Benjamin Tallmadge, being the Washington's Chief Director of Intelligence of the Culper Spy Ring, employed Robert Townsend (Samuel Culper, Jr., Agent 723) Robert Townsend's alias and the 'Culper Spy Ring' was named after Townsend's former place of employment in Culpepper, Virginia, where he has worked as a surveyor (taking the 'pep' out of the city's name). Tallmadge also hired Abraham Woodhull (whose name was changed to Samuel Culper, Sr. Agent 722). Culper Sr. had a tavern centrally located at British Headquarters, in what is today known as Manhattan, NY., where #722 befriended and mingled with British troops, then passed the 'intel' to Austin Roe (agent #724) who then carried it across New York City by horse to deliver the letters to Setauket, Long Island. There, Caleb Brewster (agent #725) brought the Intel across Long Island Sound by way of a small ferry back to Washington's Chief of Intelligence, Major Tallmadge (agent #721, who was stationed in Connecticut (735). Tallmadge then reported to General George Washington, The Fox (Agent #711).

WHILE TALLMADGE WAS keeping an eye on the inner workings and plans of the British troops, a lesser known psyops operation of Washington's was 'Haym Salomon's League of Bankers & Brokers'; who were busy befriending, extorting, and bribing the Redcoats over a protracted four-year period, between 1778 – 1783. Among those who led the covert extortion ring were Jonas Hawkins, James Rivington, Mary

Underhill, Amos Underhill, Zachariah Hawkins, Nathaniel Ruggles, John Cork, Hugh Mulligan, "Cato", Daniel Bissel, Joshua Davis and Lewis Costigin.

By 1783 Washington was notified by his two head operatives, Benjamin Tallmadge and Haym Solomon that the British stationed in and around New York were now under their full control and was able to give the French Navy the all clear to set sail for the 'New World.' When the French fleet arrived, they were, to the shock and dismay of so-called historians thereafter, with absolutely no confrontation or resistance! It was smooth sailing for the French Navy, who upon arriving just off the coast of New York's east coast, set up a Naval blockade to impede any British Naval interference. Within just a few weeks the British informally surrendered, claiming starvation for lack of supplies and ration, and departed back to Britain. The first Central Intelligence false flag attack and counterintelligence operation was a success. The elites of the Illuminati overthrew the British Army, dissolved the Church and its religious influence upon America and American Culture, making heroes of the miscreant, Atheistic and Satanic deceivers of the New World.

The Vatican controls it all!

'The deep state's plans for a Communist world Government by 2024, making the pope king!'

"The signs are increasing. The lights in the sky will appear red, blue, green, rapidly. Someone is coming from very far and wants to meet the people of the Earth. Meetings have already taken place. But those who have really seen have been silent."

- Pope John XXII, 1935

Before the advent of the New World Order in 1991 or The Order of Skull & Bones; before Freemasonry took root as a World Order and began to flourish as the hidden hand controlling all of the world as early as the 16th Century, even before the Illuminati rooted itself as a radicalized Freemasonic variant in 1776; the Vatican alone dominated the world for thousands of years. The Pope had not only been the worlds 'Holy Father', but its Shadow Government King; rooted in the Roman Empire with its tentacles of power going as far back as Roman History itself, extending throughout all of world history, predating the Greeks, Etruscans, Ancient Egypt and Babylon itself. If there has ever been a King of the world put into power without conquest, who finished the incomplete takeover of this world, which Alexander the Great had fallen short of doing, it has now been vanquished entirely by the Vatican's Pope. With all of the power upheavals that have come and gone, all of the orders of the world have united behind a bitterly fought truce of sorts under the highest of all Hierocracies, the Jesuit Order.

The Great Catholic Schism - 1054-1417

As seems to be the nature of just about everything that encompasses the 'Deep State's New World' we now live in, 'the Vatican' is also separated into two opposing groups, being theologically at war with itself. Although the original Catholic Church was born out of Rome and the Roman Empire, the founding members of the true Catholic Orthodoxy do not reside in Rome, but in eastern Europe. The Schism or breakup of the 'Greek Orthodox Church' began in 1054, primarily because of a disagreement as to whether the 'Pope' or Papacy is a Holy Father at all, as the Western European 'Holy See' believe him to be. Since 1378, The Eastern Orthodoxy has separated itself from the belief of a God-like figure who has historically referred to himself as equal to or in some cases greater than God himself.

Before this great divide, the Emperor of the Eastern Orthodoxy, (including King Charlemagne and Constantinople) have traditionally held the ultimate power in the appointment of the Pope. This is one of the primary reason's historians give us as to why there was a Great East-West Roman Catholic schism. However, it is more likely that this was just a formality in the grand scheme of things, and the real reason for the eastern Orthodoxy schism from the Vatican of the West had more to do with its intense disagreements with its Pagan Roman history, teachings, practices, and the ever-present Satanic rituals of the West, which did not bode well with their conservative Christian constituents; who still to this day, do not view the Pope as a supreme deity, but rather merely a member of their Patriarchal system. Today the Roman Catholic Church of the West seems to have more in common with the Illuminati than it does with anything traditionally Christian. The use of Iconoclasm or 'Idol worship' of the Western Orthodoxy (The Vatican) during the 8th century was seen by the Eastern Europeans, North Africans, and the Byzantine Empire as heresy and it's Idiolectic practices have been strictly condemned since the days of King Charlemagne. Their Pagan Icons, statues and images were seen as Satanic since there are many literal examples throughout the Vatican which are unequivocally of Satan. Examples of these Iconoclast images go beyond mere figurative representations of various Pagan Gods. There are murals found throughout Rome enshrined with the only intention in being to glorify Satan. These can be found covering a complete floor depicting Satan on a chariot beneath one of the many underground lairs of the Vatican. Since the very foundation of the Vatican, the Roman Statue of Jupiter was simply altered to a statue of St. Peter. A few minor adjustments made the current statue of the Virgin Mary, in Rome, out of the ancient Pagan Statue of the Roman God Venus. You can see where this may have posed a problem for those considering themselves Christians, especially during this Great Catholic Schism.

Crusades 1095-1291

The New World Order has been known to deliberately evoke the term 'Crusades' quite often, most notably during the 911 hoax or in Obama's speeches used to justify his relationship to Islam. Because the Crusades of the Middle Ages were in fact 'Holy Wars.' Yes, the same 'Holy War' term Radical Islam evokes when needed to make a rationalization for its conquest over battles necessary in the acquisition for power over Israel. The Western Roman Catholic Crusades were not only a conquest for sacred land and power, as the Vatican saw it, they were indeed the fusion of both Ancient Roman Idolatry and Islam as we know it today. Is it merely just a coincidence that after these 'Crusades,' when the Byzantine empire was vanquished by the Vatican, that many of these Roman Catholic traditions fused into the culture of Islam as we know it today? Roman Emperor, St. Augustine is just one example of how converting the Arab world to Roman Catholicism drastically changed the landscape and belief system of modern-day Islam. Over time, this became more of a fusion of a quasi-Roman Catholic/Islam. Which can be evidenced in the many similar Roman Catholic and Islamic traditions held between these two groups. Such examples can be found in the eerily similar construction of both Roman Catholic Churches and their Islamic Mosque counterparts found within feet of each other all over various cities throughout the world. How is it that two supposed diametrically opposed groups can share this space in such loving harmony? The connection of nearly identical Roman Catholic Rosary beads and Muslim prayer beads is not just striking; it is undeniable.

Islam was not the only religion touched by the hidden hand of the Roman Catholic Church, The Emperor of then Roman controlled Byzantine Empire, now North Africa, incidentally created a fusion of Roman Catholicism and 'real Christianity' which he vehemently described as a serious problem which needed to be addressed: "An anonymous document was published containing the names of many persons. Those who denied that they were or had been Christians, when they invoked the words dictated by me, offered prayer with incense and wine to your image, which I had ordered to be brought for this purpose together with statues of the gods, and moreover curse Christ, none of which those who are really Christians, it is said, can be forced to do, these I thought should be discharged. Others named by the informer declared that they were Christians, but then denied it, asserting that they had been but had ceased to be, some three years before, others many years, some as much as twenty-five years, they all worshipped your image and the statues of the Gods and cursed Christ. They asserted, however, that the sum and substance of their fault or error had been that they were accustomed to meet on a fixed day before dawn and sing responsively a hymn to Christ as a god, and to bind themselves by oath, not to some crime, but not to commit, fraud, theft, or adultery, not falsify their trust, nor to refuse to return a trust when called upon to do so. When this was over, it was their custom to depart and to assemble again to partake of food - but ordinary and innocent food. Even this, they affirmed, they had ceased to do after my edict by which, in accordance with your instructions, I had forbidden political associations. Accordingly, I judged it all the more necessary to find out what the truth was by torturing two female slaves who were called deaconesses. But I discovered nothing else but depraved, excessive superstition."

- Letter to Governor Pliny to Emperor Trajan addressing the Roman Catholic Conquest

Regarding the Roman Catholic conquest of the Arab world, historian and excommunicated Jesuit Priest (by his own volition) describes an account of The Vatican's creation of Islam itself:

"Looking to North Africa, they saw the multitudes of Arabs as a source of manpower to do their dirty work. A number of Arabs had become Roman Catholic and could be used in reporting information to their leaders in Rome. Others could be used as a Fifth Column (an underground spy network) to carry out Rome's master plan to control the great multitudes of Arabs who had completely rejected Roman Catholicism. The Vatican wanted to create a messiah for the Arabs, someone they could raise up as a great leader, a man with charisma whom they could train, and eventually unite all the non-Catholic Arabs behind him, creating a mighty army that would ultimately capture Jerusalem for the pope." - Former Jesuit Priest, Alberto Rivera

Protestant Reformation 1517-1648

Some would argue that there is a third sect of the Catholic Church, being Protestant of the Lutheran ilk of the Vatican's 'Holy See.' This, of course, is a fallacy since the Protestants have not only vehemently opposed the Roman Catholic Church altogether 1517, but have fought brutally savage and bloody wars over their departure from it, bringing their reformed way of life to the 'New World' to permanently escape it.

All agents of the Vatican must take the Vatican Oath:

THE OATH I_____ , now in the presence of Almighty God, the blessed Virgin Mary, the blessed St. John the Baptist, the Holy Apostles, St. Peter and St. Paul, and all the saints, sacred host of heaven, and to you, my Ghostly Father, the superior general of the Society of Jesus founded by St. Ignatius Loyola, in the pontification of Paul the III and continued to the present, do by the womb of the Virgin, the matrix of God, and the rod of Jesus Christ, declare and swear that His Holiness the Pope, is Christ's vice regent and is the true and only head of the Catholic or Universal Church throughout the earth; and that by virtue of the keys of binding and loosing given His Holiness by my Savior, Jesus Christ, he hath power to depose heretical kings, princes, States, Commonwealths, and Governments and they may be safely destroyed. Therefore to the utmost of my power I will defend this doctrine and His Holiness's right and custom against all usurpers of the heretical or Protestant authority whatever, especially the Lutheran Church of Germany, Holland, Denmark, Sweden, and Norway and the now pretended authority and Churches of England and Scotland, and the branches of same now established in Ireland and on the Continent of America and elsewhere, and all adherents in regard that they may be usurped and heretical, opposing the sacred Mother Church of Rome. I do now denounce and disown any allegiance as due to any heretical king, prince, or State, named Protestant or Liberals, or obedience to any of their laws, magistrates, or officers. I do further declare that the doctrine of the Churches of England and Scotland, of the Calvinists, Huguenots, and others of the name of Protestants or Masons to be damnable, and they themselves to be damned who will not forsake the same. I do further declare that I will help assist, and advise all or any of His Holiness's agents, in any place where I should be, in Switzerland, Germany, Holland, Ireland, or America, or in any other kingdom or territory I shall come to and do my utmost to extirpate the heretical Protestant or Masonic doctrines and to destroy all their pretended powers, legal or otherwise. I do further promise and declare that, notwithstanding I am dispensed with to assume any religion heretical for the propagation of the Mother Church's interest to keep secret and private all her agents' counsels from time to time, as they entrust me and not divulge, directly or indirectly, by word, writing, or circumstances whatever but to execute all that should be proposed, given in charge or discovered unto me by you my Ghostly father, or any of this sacred order. I do further promise and declare that I will have no opinion or will of my own or any mental reservation whatsoever, even as a corpse or cadaver (perindeac cadaver), but will unhesitatingly obey each and every command that I may receive from my superiors in the militia of the Pope and of Jesus Christ. That I will go to any part of the world whithersoever I may be sent, to the frozen regions north, jungles of India, to the centers of civilization of Europe, or to the wild haunts of the barbarous savages of America without murmuring or repining, and will be submissive in all things whatsoever is communicated to me. I do further promise and declare that I will, when opportunity presents, make and wage relentless war, secretly and openly against all heretics, Protestants, and Masons, as I am directed to do to extirpate them from the face of the whole earth; and that I will spare neither age, sex, or condition, and that will hang, burn, waste, boil, flay, strangle, and bury alive these infamous heretics; rip up the stomachs and wombs of their women, and crush their infants' heads against the walls in order to annihilate their execrable race. That when the same cannot be done openly, I will secretly use the poisonous cup, the strangulation cord, the steel of the poniard, or the leaden bullet, regardless of the honor, rank, dignity, or authority of the persons, whatever may be their condition in life, either public or private, as I at any time may be directed so to do by any agents of the Pope or superior of the Brotherhood of the Holy Father of the Society of Jesus. In confirmation of which I hereby dedicate my life, soul, and all corporal powers, and with the dagger which I now receive I will subscribe my name written in my blood in testimony thereof; and should I prove false or weaken in my determination, may my brethren and fellow soldiers of the militia of the Pope cut off my hands and feet and my throat from ear to ear, my belly opened and Sulphur burned therein with all the punishment that can be inflicted upon me on earth and my soul shall be tortured by demons in eternal hell forever. That I will in voting always vote for a K. of C. in preference to a Protestant, especially a Mason, and that I will leave my party so to do; that if two Catholics are on the ticket, I will satisfy myself which is the better supporter of Mother Church and vote accordingly. That I will not deal with or employ a Protestant if in my power to deal with or employ a Catholic. That I will place Catholic girls in Protestant families that a weekly report may be made of the inner movements of the heretics. That I will provide myself with arms and ammunition that I may be in readiness when the word is passed, or I am commanded to defend the church either as an individual or with the militia of the Pope. All of which I, _____, do swear by the blessed Trinity and blessed sacrament which I am now to receive to perform and on part to keep this, my oath. In testimony hereof, I take this most holy and blessed Sacrament of the Eucharist and witness the same further with my name written with the point of this dagger dipped in my own blood and seal in the face of this sacrament.

"*Anybody who is acquainted with the state of affairs in the Vatican in the last 35 years is well aware that the prince of darkness has and still has his surrogates in the court of St. Peter in Rome. Untold numbers of outright Satan worshippers are now masquerading as Catholic clergy while secretly paying homage to Lucifer. It has gotten so bad that in one shocking incident, high-ranking churchmen actually took oaths signed with their own blood and participated in meticulously enacted rituals that blaspheme and devilishly mimic the holy sacrifice of the mass.*"

- Catholic scholar Dr. Malachi Martin, The Fatima Crusade

If a picture is truly worth a thousand words, as the old adage goes, then the picture below of a young Pope Benedict the XVI (Joseph Alois Ratzinger) giving a hail Hitler solute below, the picture of Hitler's meeting with Pope Pius the XII and the one near the bottom of a Nazi SS and Vatican meeting should speak volumes on their own.

The Concord of 1933 was the official alliance signed between the Vatican and Nazi Germany. History has a difficult time recounting the various Vatican Pope's who not only participated with

Nazi Germany during the Second World War, but also completely fueled, fomented and funded it with the help of the Vatican! Hitler did not work on his own, he answered to, you guessed it, the Pope! Hitler was born and raised Roman Catholic with a membership in the Jesuit Order! This is also very difficult for many people to accept especially since Adolf Hitler was also a known occultist and Satanist who participated in the slaughter and extermination of Jews, gays, Soviet POW's and many more innocent people amounting to 18 million deaths, all told.

There are a web of secret societies which are not just in America but span the globe. They are international, and some are more well known, like 'The Order of Death,' (A.K.A. Skull & Bones) while some are simply a conglomerate of businesses, such as The Bilderberg Group, many of whom are not even aware that they too are 'Secret Society' members. These secret societies do not display

flashing neon lights with the words 'Deep State' written at their headquarters - or they would not be so secret after all. Instead, many of them are law firms that can be found throughout the country; some are now 'Federal' Agencies, Churches, Temples, Mosques, Synagogues, Cable News outlets, Television Networks, Film Studios, etc. However, the cities and towns you live in most likely have some connection to this vast global enterprise and oftentimes those same cities were named just to let you know who's running this 'New World.' It doesn't matter which country you live in; the Deep State has a hand in every one of them. Iran and North Korea were the only two countries left who were not, until recently, but they too have also always been 'Satellite States' of the New World

Order. If you think you are immune to the Deep State, think again. Chances are you are already a part of it. Unfortunately, until this system is properly dismantled, we are all a part of this nefarious Deep State which has taken thousands of years to build. There are only two warring factions of the Deep State, the Illuminati and the Vatican.

Both are incredibly powerful and own and completely control all of the lesser known and more elusive Secret Societies who independently and locally govern the world. The irony in having two warring groups inside of a Deep State is that both have strong disagreements about the Separation of a Church and State in Government. The Vatican has generally been a Theocracy, ruling Governments by religious authority. What else could they be, with a Pope at the top of its world hierarchy? The Illumination the other hand has always claimed to be seeking refuge from this very same 'despotic and tyrannical' Vatican imposed Theatrocractic system of world Governance. They claim to have a need to escape religious persecution, but is the Vatican religious at all? The American settlers were however actually escaping religious persecution from the Vatican's despotic 'Church.' The Pilgrims came to America, aboard the Mayflower in 1620. The Puritans, Lutherans and Protestant Church followed in this pursuit of a less intrusive American land to settle upon, not necessarily interested in a Government at all; nor were these religious groups thinking about who would eventually control the New World which they chose to settle upon. They were content just being free from the Vatican's despotic rule over the rest of the world. When the founding fathers mention a 'Separation of Church and State', they were speaking in general terms, sometimes eluding to 'the Church of England', but the idea that there was any other 'Church' at that time, other than the Vatican's Roman Catholic Church, is not only misleading but completely false. As far as Governments are concerned, the world has only known one despotic and tyrannical Church, the Vatican! Had they foreseen some other 'Church' more powerful than the Roman Catholic's Vatican-State, there was no mention or implication of it, but to the present day, the Vatican rules it all! Therefore, we can safely assume that the founding fathers 'Separation of Church and State' reference found in the Bill of Rights and the Constitution were specifically focusing on the 'Holy Roman Empire's Catholic Church.'

Both the Freemason's and Illuminati, both of which nearly every American 'founding father' were members of in degrees, have always maintained an extreme and vehement opposition to the Vatican and its tyrannical System over the people of the world. This is also why these two warring groups (one religious, the other claiming no religious affiliation) they appear to be at odds with each other. But why is there no mention of a Separation of Societies and State or despotic groups and State? After all, a Society has the ability to become equal to or greater in power than any Church, does it not? It is a valid question to pose especially considering the fact that in 1776 the Vatican was a Church, but the implication of being a Church based in religion is implied; since the very word 'Church' evokes the idea of some sort of religion based in a Christian God. Yet there is no mention of any exclusion of Ideologically driven groups, such as the Freemason's or the Illuminati or any other 'Secret Societies' from the State. The only reference made of any Separation of Powers in the Constitution is regarding a religious one, "Congress shall make no law respecting an establishment of religion, or prohibiting the free exercise thereof."

It seems logical to assume that the founding fathers were doing us a service in giving us freedom of Religion, which they did out of necessity, but we cannot ignore the more significant implications of the Enlightenment Era's Ideological foundation which was built on the premise that the there is no God, and we are free and liberal; and beyond that, going deeper these so-called enlightenment/socialist thinkers, like Rousseau and Voltaire, were not the self-ascribed atheists who opposed God which they attempted to portray themselves as, they were literal Luciferian and Satan-worshiping haters of God. This is why Separation of Church and State has more to do with controlling the masses of Americans not to be religious at all, nor to be Christians than it has to do with any sort of Freedom from oppressive Government.

Here's where it gets somewhat confusing, why have the Vatican and the Illuminati/Freemasons been so diametrically and vehemently opposed to one another for almost 600 years, when they both share many of the same ideological beliefs for a Luciferian New World? The answer is that the Vatican created the Illuminati and Freemasonry was because whatever it cannot control, it simply modifies itself to suit the needs of any particular ideological group. In the case of Non-Christians, the only way to maintain any semblance of Order in the 'New World' was to give them Freemasonry and the Illuminati. In doing so, the Vatican was now in a position where it could have dominance over their 'Christians,' through the Vatican's

Church-State, while subsequently maintaining Supremacy over the non-believers, atheist and even Satanists of the world.

Just as the Vatican has unsuccessfully attempted to convert various aspects of Christianity, the Eastern Orthodoxy, the Arab World, and Judaism to Roman Catholicism; wherever it has not been successful in its conversion, instead of forcing them into submission to their version of the Vatican's Roman Catholic Church, they simply either leave it alone or create a new religion based on the principles of the Jesuit Order thereby maintaining control. The Vatican has used this same principle during the 'Crusades' giving the Arab world the illusion of freedom, in the creation of Islam, while simultaneously maintaining control of that region of the world.

The Vatican is its very own Country, has a membership with the United Nations (which it controls), it is also the most powerful Bank in the world. It is the religious epicenter of the world and has created and maintained control over all political groups and its representatives. It has even created its very own opposition to itself, the Illuminati/Freemasonry; all in an effort to manipulate every side of all warring countries, religions, groups and 'Secret Societies' of the world. All of the highest ranking of the most prominent members of the most powerful Secret Societies answer to them. However, it seems that because of the utter and complete secrecy of some of these groups, there has been a communications breakdown over the course of the last 250 years, and the Illuminati/Freemasons may have fallen out of touch with the Vatican as a result of this.

However, in recent decades, beginning around 1991, this communication breakdown, its power struggles and upheavals over time have seemed to come to an end; Both the Vatican and the Illuminati have come to an understanding that they were born of the same mother and any infighting amongst each other runs contrary to their world agenda. The New World Order is the ultimate of all orders mentioned in this book because it combines all 'Orders', new and old, throughout the world, working proactively together despite their differences towards their shared common goal of a One-world Government and a complete New World Order with its very own world Dictator and King: The Pope. In accordance with the New World Order's writings, the Pope is to become King of this One-World-Government sometime between 2023 and 2030. The Deep State can be defeated, but it will take more than the miracle of Trump's Presidency to come to fruition. The end of the Deep State can only completely take place with God's divine intervention!

SANDY HOOK, THE CIA, The White House, DOD, the Library of Congress, the Supreme Court, and you guessed it, the Pentagon all line up with the '33rd Parallel of death', which is a ley-line or 'global line' that begins from the North, at Stonehenge, and extends southward along the U.S. eastern seaboard to its southernmost

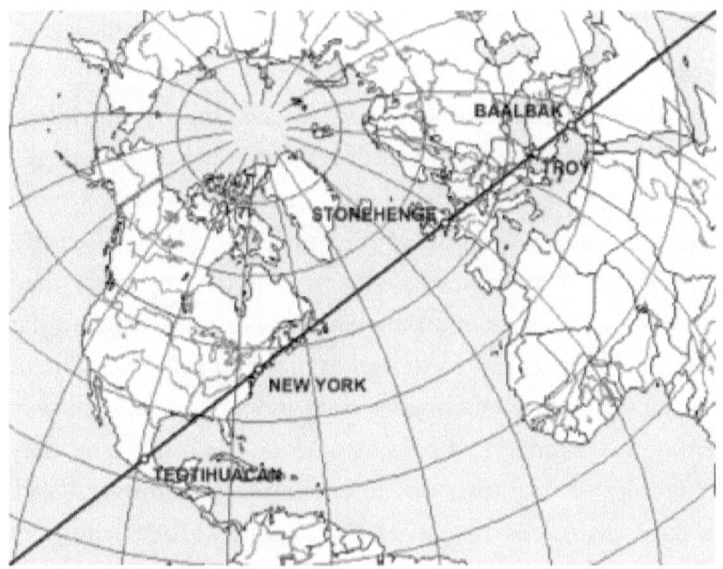

point at Teotihuacan, Mexico, 5,458 miles away. The 'Sirius Ley-Line' (not pictured here) intersects with this 33rd Parallel ley-line extending through Houston, Texas (JFK assassination) as it passes through Memphis, Tennessee (MLK assassination), into Japan. This 'Sirius ley-line' is also known as the 'Arcadia Meridian' and it is also believed to have intersecting points that form a man-made, Freemasonic grid or triangle of Sacrifice that does not coincidentally begin and end at Stonehenge and Teotihuacan, Mexico's Temple of Quetzalcoatl at the Pyramid of the Sun and Moon or 'The Avenue of Death'. The Romans celebrated it at Stonehenge after conquering the Gaul's who began the tradition before them, beginning the celebration on May 1st through the 15th, Witches Day, A.K.A. the festivity of the Shrine to 'Vulcan'. Of course, these human sacrificial rituals have always been celebrated, most notably at the sacrificial stone of these Megalithic stone structures—made by

Freemasonic-Druids and pre-Aztec pagans at the Teotihuacan's Temple of Quetzalcoatl!

Is the 33rd Meridian a sacrificial line honoring a six-thousand-year-old tradition of human sacrifice with Pagan and Satanic roots that span nearly six-thousand miles from Stonehenge to the Pyramid of the Sun? Were the Druids and the pre-Aztecan civilization, who have both long since died out, working together in an ancient Globalized world similar to today's? If so was this by design or merely a coincidence? An understanding of recent history does in fact hold the answer. Freemasons do indeed wish to bring back the one whom they call the 'Grand Architect of the Universe'; to summon 'God' back to earth to recreate what they herald to be 'the age of wisdom' to fuse the scientific and the metaphysical, ideally under a one-world Government.

The Secret History of the 'Brotherhood of the Diamond'

As has been clearly stated, the architects of Masonry and its roots were established long before any of its earliest known records were discovered or upon its formal inception in 1623 The Freemason globalized philosophy has reshaped the function of science, mathematics, the educational system worldwide, all governments, its leaders, politicians, elites, secret societies, nearly every religious institution (international and local), and even the geographical landscape and positioning of many of the major cities throughout the world. Masons are not only the architects of buildings, they have been the architects of our world, lurking behind everything imaginable which now encompasses it.

The hero of the Freemasons is a metaphorical character named Hiram Abiff who is at the heart of all Masonic teachings, and is believed by those who practice its rites to be the architect of King Solomon's Temple. Although Biblical scholars denounce this belief as heresy, since no actual reference to this man is mentioned in the Torah or Bible, a great many Masons believe Hiram Abiff was a literal person and not figurative at all. Critics of this belief argue that Hiram is the Masons very own Jesus Christ, created simply to suit the needs of their Secret Society.

As the legend goes, Hyrum Abiff is the Widow's son, the master builder of King Solomon's temple. The Widow is believed by some to signify Mary, the mother of Jesus. Since Mary was married to Joseph, there would be no conceivable reason for Mary to be a widow unless Masons hold the belief that Mary is the wife of a dead father (Since Jesus is considered to be 'The Son of God' by Judeo-Christians, this Freemasonic analogy could only mean the son of a dead God). According to the legend of King Solomon was given the design and dimensions of his temple directly from God and Hyrum Abiff, its master builder, was the only other man who knew of its secret design, power and secrets which it held. Abiff (Masonic-Jesus) is then threatened by three men ('the three wise men', Ignorance, fanaticism and Tyranny) who demanded the secret knowledge behind King Solomon's Temple. The Three Mason builders of the Temple believe there was a code word that carries God's divine plan and that if they are able to receive the code will also receive Divine or magical God-like powers. The Three Stone cutters ask Hyrum for the secret word for months and are not given an answer, so finally, as Abiff approaches the east door of the Temple to pray; one of the three men accost him demanding the Secret. According to the legend, Hyrum Abiff tells him that they will be given it when they have accomplished their work, and the Temple is complete. Hyrum's throat is then cut with the Masons stone, when the second builder demands 'the word', again Abiff refuses to give the secret and is then struck with the Mason's Square. The Third Mason asks yet again and is refused, this time Abiff is killed with another Square. As he's dying, he yells, 'who will help the widow's son?'

The rituals, indoctrination, and initiation in the Freemasonry, or the 'Brotherhood of the Diamond' (Incidentally, the mystery of the Diamond is perhaps the most hidden of all Freemasonic secrets, but is important to understand, since the Pyramids are associated with Freemasons - their ever-present Pyramidal symbols and Washington D.C.'s boundaries do not form a square, but a Diamond!) all center around the theme of Hiram Abiff legend. The purpose given by Freemasons for the importance of this metaphorical teaching put into practice with Masonic garb and regalia, fake beards, and costumes etc. is one, to stress importance of 'Death before Dishonor '; and secondly, to imitate the rebirth of its initiates being reborn, as Jesus Christ, but instead by Hiram Abiff, welcoming their members into a pre-Illuminati World Order

THESIS

The origins of Stone Masonry began with the first King of England, King Athelstan in the 10th century A.D. These Stone Masons were not merely stone cutters who decided to claim freedom from the Church, quite the opposite, they were very much the Church itself; bound with a very real interlock with the Roman Catholic Church, as they are today with the Jesuit-Catholic Church of the Vatican. They were the founding fathers, so to speak, of modern Masonry today, hence the derivation of their name Freemasons. The idea of fusing Democratic-Socialism, Metaphysical Mysticism with the hard science of Geometry, and Kabalistic mathematics has now become the cornerstone, if you will of modern-day Freemasonry. By the late 1700's the conditions were ripe for an Adam Weishaupt to overhaul and radicalize the already extreme world of the Freemasons, bringing the Masons deeper into the full-blown practice of Satanism, no longer being shrouded in mystical teachings and what the Masons like to call 'their journey'. As explained in Volume I of the History of the Deep State, the Order of the Illuminati made no 'bones' about what they believed was truly at the heart of Masonry, with the new order of Weishaupt being established and accepted at every Freemasonic Temple and lodge around the world by 1776 and extending into the second Order of Death, with the advent of Skull and Bones in 1832, then at last being perfected and ushered into the New World Order in 1991; when the Secret of the brotherhood of the Diamond was finally put to rest, being fully exposed in plain sight!

JEREMY STONE

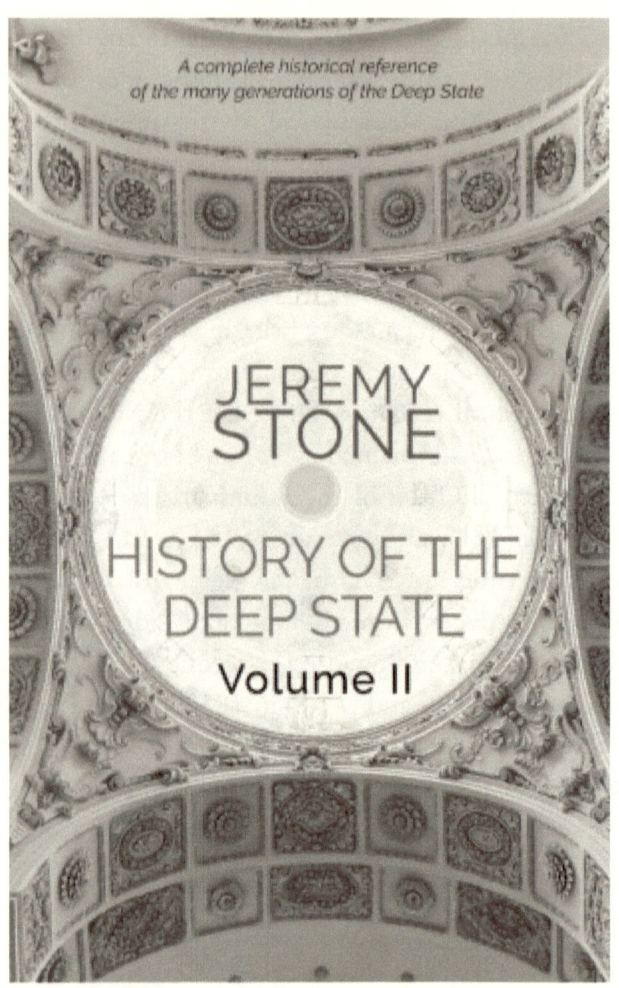

A complete historical reference
of the many generations of the Deep State

JEREMY
STONE

HISTORY OF THE
DEEP STATE
Volume II

THE HISTORY OF THE DEEP STATE: VOLUME II
OF THE HISTORY OF DEEP STATE TRILOGY!!!

YOU WILL ALSO LOVE 'THE DEEP STATE: THE NOVEL', ALSO THE FIRST OF A DEEP STATE SERIES OF FANTASTIC THRILLERS!!!

"The very word "secrecy" is repugnant in a free and open society; and we are as a people inherently and historically opposed to secret societies, to secret oaths and to secret proceedings. We decided long ago that the dangers of excessive and unwarranted concealment of pertinent facts far outweighed the dangers which are cited to justify it. Even today, there is little value in opposing the threat of a closed society by imitating its arbitrary restrictions. Even today, there is little value in insuring the survival of our nation if our traditions do not survive with it. And there is very grave danger that an announced need for increased security will be seized upon by those anxious to expand its meaning to the very limits of official censorship and concealment. That I do not intend to permit to the extent that it is in my control. And no official of my Administration, whether his rank is high or low, civilian or military, should interpret my words here tonight as an excuse to censor the news, to stifle dissent, to cover up our mistakes or to withhold from the press and the public the facts they deserve to know.

But I do ask every publisher, every editor, and every newsman in the nation to reexamine his own standards, and to recognize the nature of our country's peril. In time of war, the government and the press have customarily joined in an effort based largely on self-discipline, to prevent unauthorized disclosures to the enemy. In time of "clear and present danger," the courts have held that even the privileged rights of the First Amendment must yield to the public's need for national security.

Today no war has been declared—and however fierce the struggle may be, it may never be declared in the traditional fashion. Our way of life is under attack. Those who make themselves our enemy are advancing around the globe. The survival of our friends is in danger. And yet no war has been declared, no borders have been crossed by marching troops, no missiles have been fired. If the press is awaiting a declaration of war before it imposes the self-discipline of combat conditions, then I can only say that no war ever posed a greater threat to our security. If you are awaiting a finding of "clear and present danger," then I can only say that the danger has never been more clear, and its presence has never been more imminent.

It requires a change in outlook, a change in tactics, a change in missions—by the government, by the people, by every businessman or labor leader, and by every newspaper. For we are opposed around the world by a monolithic and ruthless conspiracy that relies primarily on covert means for expanding its sphere of influence—on infiltration instead of invasion, on subversion instead of elections, on intimidation instead of free choice, on guerrillas by night instead of armies by day. It is a system which has conscripted vast human and material resources into the building of a tightly knit, highly efficient machine that combines military, diplomatic, intelligence, economic, scientific and political operations.

Its preparations are concealed, not published. Its mistakes are buried, not headlined. Its dissenters are silenced, not praised. No expenditure is questioned, no rumor is printed, no secret is revealed."

- President John F. Kennedy, 1961

JEREMY STONE

Drain The Deep State!

#MAGA